An-Ya

安雅

An-Ya
and Her Diary

A NOVEL BY

Diane René Christian

For my daughters

安雅

My pen is finally touching your pages. It is time to tell our story. Our story began in China and now it continues in America. I want to write about our old life and I want to write about our life now. I will write it all down with hopes that somehow I can connect the two worlds that I have lived in. Right now those worlds seem so far apart. I don't know if it is possible for my world to ever feel whole, without a crack down the middle...but it is time to try.

1

Dear Diary,

All that She left inside the box was a blank book and a name. You are the book, and I am the name...An-Ya. As you know, my name is printed on your first page. Did She write it? What did She look like as She stood over you with Her pen? Were there tears in Her eyes? Why were you left empty inside?

I wish you could speak to me. You have too many secrets. You remember Her putting us in the box. You remember how far She carried us. As we lay beneath the red gate, did we stare into the sun or stars? Did I cry? Did She cry?

Why can't you answer me? I don't like that about you. These are my secrets to share and not yours to keep inside these blank pages. It is not fair. It's not fair at all.

You and She are a lot alike. All mysteries and no answers. She made a terrible decision leaving you empty, because it left me empty too.

2

Dear Diary,

You and I have been together all of my life. We waited together. In China I waited for Her to come back. If a stranger entered the orphanage, I was sure it was Her. Or maybe She was sick, or maybe She died, and He would come. I studied every person that came in. I knew They were coming back. I was so sure. But They didn't come. We watched baby after baby find their home before us. Everyone wanted the babies. I kept growing and growing, and every day I was less special than the day before. People loved the babies. I never stopped hoping for Them to return for me. But nobody wanted me there, not even Them. I should have stopped hoping. It would have been easier that way.

Instead of Them, strangers, who look nothing like me, came from the other side of the world. They came to take me away from China forever. If She returned, then I would be gone. Maybe I was happy to know that someone wanted me. Maybe I was sad that I would be lost to Them forever. Maybe I was angry that it didn't matter what I thought because other people decided for me. Maybe I felt all of these things and so much more.

We flew to the other side of the world, and I never stopped holding you close to my chest. You were empty and so was I. My only friend in the world. The only one who understood where I began and where I was going. We flew together and everything we knew before was gone.

3

Dear Diary,

I have a new mother and a father. I call my father Daddy. I call my mother Wanna. I call her that in secret because she *Wanna* be my mommy. She can't. They mean nothing to me. I know their names, I know how many papers they signed to make me their daughter, but those papers mean nothing. I don't have anything else to say about them right now.

4

Dear Diary,

I have a sister now. Her name is Ellie. She was adopted from China as a baby, and now she is 3 years old. She was one of the special babies that left the orphanage over and over. Actually, she is not that special. She doesn't remember anything about China. She makes up fake stories and thinks that they are real. She forgot China. I didn't forget. I remember my life in China. My new parents think that she is wonderful. I don't care what they think, because they will never know how special I am. I will never share my life with them and I will only tell you. Only you will understand the whole story. I will fill your emptiness and that will be enough.

5

Dear Diary,

I gained a family and I lost a family. Forever. They never came and I was taken to America. I wanted to go back. I hated everything about my new life. Nobody looked like me, the food tasted awful, and worst of all was the night. I had never slept alone before, except maybe during my time in the box. I don't know how long I was in the box before I was found. But after that, I never slept alone. I was always surrounded by rows of sleeping children waiting just like me. I was used to the sounds of crying, coughing, snoring, and sneezing. It was my night music in the orphanage. America was too quiet.

My new family put me in a room by myself. All alone. I couldn't tell them that I was afraid. I couldn't speak. I knew the English words. I learned them in China. The problem was that the English words wouldn't come out. I only knew how to scream. I screamed outside my new parents' bedroom door. I never screamed in China. I don't know what happened to me. I screamed and cried, and they kept taking me back to my room. Over and over. Night after night. Finally one day, I gave up. My pillow was always wet. I hated the night and I still hate the night.

6

Dear Diary,

You are probably wondering why I waited so long to write in you. For eleven years I have held you and stared at your red cover and looked at your empty pages. You are covered in gold flowers. I have counted them many times. They are beautiful. You are beautiful.

I thought maybe She had a plan when she left you with me. I thought Her plan was for me to keep you empty until She came back for us. I know it doesn't make sense. She didn't leave me a plan, so now I need a plan of my own.

Sorry I waited so long.

By the way, I gave you a name. I named you Penny. I am filling your pages with Pen. Nobody can erase you. Nobody can make you empty again.

7

Dear Penny,

Do you remember the little girl in the orphanage with the white hair and grey eyes? I don't know how you could forget her. She was with us all of the time. I remember everything about her, but for some reason I can't remember her name. Her name sounded something like—Abby. It makes my head hurt to try and remember her name. Why can't I remember her name?

I do remember that she was an annoying little girl. She followed me everywhere and held onto my shirt wherever we walked. Her eyes didn't work well. Sometimes one eye would go the wrong direction.

When she came in to the orphanage, she would not let the nannies feed her a bottle. Only I could give her the bottle. She would not touch anybody but me. If I didn't feed her with a bottle, then she wouldn't eat.

Abby would grab my shirt and not let go all day. Do you know how annoying it is to have someone holding your shirt all day? Sometimes I pushed her to get her off me. Sometimes I pushed her down. But she always got back up and grabbed back on.

If I wanted to get rid of her, I would go outside to play. She wasn't allowed outside in the sun. Sometimes I would get tired of her and go outside. Abby would sit inside the door and wait for me to come back in. She is probably still sitting there. Waiting. I didn't say goodbye because I was happy to have her off of my shirt. I should have told her I wasn't coming back. She is probably still sitting next to the orphanage door, waiting for me to come back and starving.

8

Dear Penny,

I found out I was going to America when a nanny came to get me and took me to meet an English teacher. I asked why I was meeting an English teacher, and she said it was because I would need to be able to talk to my American family. There wasn't any time to think about it, or time to ask more questions, because she walked me down the hall and pushed me into a room. There was nothing in the room except for a desk, a chair, and a Chinese man. I walked into the room and put you under the chair and sat down. There were no windows to look out, just the man standing over me. He wasn't nice to look at either.

The man, my teacher, told me to sit down and to listen closely. He was not a nice man, not at all. He told me that my American family was paying him to teach me English and he would be coming every day. He said I would have a lot of homework to do. The teacher said it was his job to show the American family that he was an excellent teacher. If I didn't learn, then he would look like a bad teacher. So he said I better pay attention or he would smack me. I believed him and I always paid attention.

Many months went by, and over and over I repeated English words and wrote English words. I walked around the orphanage, Abby hanging on my shirt, and named every object I could find with the English word. *Chair, light, wall, shoe, toilet, door.* It wasn't long before I knew more words than I could count. Sometimes Abby would try to speak in English too. It was like a game to her. It wasn't a game to me. It was going to be my life.

One day the English teacher didn't come. My American family came instead. I'm tired of writing. I am going to put the pen down now.

9

Dear Penny,

I was thinking about the day that I first saw my American family. The first time I saw them was in a photo that they sent to the orphanage. A nanny gave me the photo and a letter from them. I didn't read the letter for a long time because I was too busy looking at the picture.

They looked different than I imagined they would look. The picture was taken next to a lake. It is the lake that we go to now almost every day. I was surprised to see a little Chinese girl in the picture. She was too small and happy, and I knew I wasn't going to like her very much.

Wanna and Daddy looked happy too. Wanna's hair was yellow like the sun and her face was round. She was much smaller than Daddy. His hair was black and he was much bigger than Wanna. He looked like he was the nicest. His smile wasn't as big as Wanna and my new sister, but he didn't look mean either. Plus, his hair was black. Maybe it wasn't Chinese black, but it was dark. At least something about him was the same.

10

Dear Penny,

My house is light brown on the outside and old on the inside. The floors are wood and there is a fireplace in almost every room. When your feet hit the wood floor, it makes the floor talk. If you are going somewhere in secret, then you need to walk on your tiptoes.

Some fireplaces don't work anymore. The one in my room doesn't work, but the living room and kitchen fireplaces do. On cool nights Daddy will put wood in the fireplace. Sometimes, even on the hottest days, the night will be cold.

I like to sit next to the fireplaces and watch the wood burn. I am not allowed to sit too close, but I sit close enough that my whole body is warm and glows orange.

There are trees all around the house, and they are the brightest green that I ever saw. Beneath the trees is grass that is almost as green as the trees. From my window I can see the blue lake. It takes a long time to walk there, but from my window it doesn't seem so far away.

11

Dear Penny,

When I was in the orphanage, I read the letter from my new family. I remember that I was scared to read it and I know that I waited. The photo was already too hard to look at. I was nervous about the letter.

I do remember being confused after I finally read the letter. It was filled with things that couldn't be true. My American family said that they loved me, that they couldn't wait to hold me, that they missed me, that they thought I was beautiful.

I knew that they couldn't feel these things because they didn't know me yet. I knew that they imagined a daughter that I was not going to be. I wanted to believe what they said, but I was too smart to believe it. I knew too much, and I knew the badness inside of me that they would hate.

12

Dear Penny,

Do you know why I carry you everywhere? It is to keep you safe. I do a good job keeping you safe. Do you remember the Nanny in the orphanage who told me she would throw you away if I didn't behave? I hated her. I will always hold on to you so that nobody can throw you away. Ever. I carry you everywhere, and I don't care if I look strange with a book under my arm or not.

13

Dear Penny,

Do you like going to the lake? I don't know if I like it. I don't like living in the middle of nowhere. There are trees and trees and trees on and on forever. And water. Wanna takes me and my sister, Ellie, to the lake to swim on hot days. There is sand on the lake shore, just like the ocean. Well, I guess it's like the ocean because I have never been to a real beach. This is a lake beach and the water is still. I would like to swim in ocean waves someday.

In China I watched a movie that showed children playing in the ocean. They were on a vacation. The water was light blue. The children were happy. They jumped up and down in the ocean waves. I think that I would like to feel a big wave wash over me.

The lake here is like a gigantic bath tub. The water is too quiet. I don't know what to do when it is so quiet. It makes me nervous. I think an ocean wave crashing over me would feel better. My sister Ellie likes the lake.

14

Dear Penny,

Ellie loves dresses. I don't. She wears a different dress every day. She thinks that she is a princess. I know I am not a princess and I wear pants. Wanna does not know how to dress her children. In China I would never be able to go outside in just a dress. Well, I never had a dress, but if I did, then I would need to wear more things to keep me warm. Sometimes in the orphanage, I would wear two or three pairs of pants and two or three shirts. Plus a jacket and sometimes a hat.

Wanna is not keeping Ellie safe. My sister never says that she is cold, but I know that she needs to wear more clothes. I have a lot of clothes now. I also have dresses in my closet. Too many. Those dresses won't keep me safe. Most of the time I wear the only clothes that the orphanage gave me. They feel the best against my skin. Not too soft and a little bit scratchy. In China I wore my clothes for many days before they were washed. Wanna wants to wash them every day.

15

Dear Penny,

The first place that I visited after we came home was the lake. The second was the market and ice cream parlor. If I walk one way from my house, I go to the lake. If I walk the other way, I end up at the market and parlor.

The market is small but has everything we need inside. It is where Wanna buys a lot of our food. A door inside the market opens into the ice cream parlor. There is a counter with red stools and three red benches on either side. I like to sit on the stools, and I place you on the counter next to my ice cream bowl. We get to choose the flavor and I always get vanilla. Ellie tries something different every time we go.

The girl who works in the ice cream parlor is really pretty. Her name is Jasmine, but her friends call her Jazz. She has a lot of girlfriends and even some boyfriends. Her hair is long and dark brown. Jazz never wears dresses. She has pants with little diamonds on the pockets.

I like to listen to Jazz and her friends talk. I spend the whole time in the parlor eating and listening. It is like they have a secret language, and they use words that Wanna and Daddy don't use. Jazz and her friends talk in a special way.

16

Dear Penny,

Shhhhh. I woke up. It is very late. I had a bad dream. I heard the children calling for me. I heard the voices of the children in the orphanage. They were screaming for me. They were crying so hard. I couldn't go back to them. I couldn't find the door to get into the orphanage. There were no doors. They needed me. They needed to eat. They were hungry. They wanted me to sing to them. They wanted to play. I played with them, although sometimes I played in a mean way. They didn't care. They wanted me back. I left them. How could I leave them? They needed me.
I can't sleep anymore.

17

Dear Penny,

Don't lose your Chinese. That is what the nannies told me. Why did they tell me that? Why did they care? They said don't forget. I am forgetting.

18

Dear Penny,

Wanna asked me to draw a picture today. It was a picture of my head. She told me to put inside my head the colors and shapes that showed how my head was feeling right now. Ellie drew a picture of her head too. Inside my head drawing, I put black and red circles. I don't know why. That is what I felt like doing. It didn't mean anything. What I wanted to draw was a big fire inside my head because that is how it really feels. Ellie put pink and purple princess crowns inside her head. I should have told her that the crown goes on top of a head, not inside of it. I didn't say anything.

19

Dear Penny,

American toilets are stupid. The first time I used one was in a hotel in China. Our adoption guide showed me how to use it. I told her—

Yes, yes, I got it, I got it.

But I didn't really get it, and I was sure that I was going to fall in or fall off. I still don't like American toilets. What is the point of a tall toilet anyway? Chinese toilets, with the hole in the ground, make much more sense.

20

Dear Penny,

Wanna is crazy and she is making me crazy too. She won't stop asking me questions. She wants me to share how I am feeling.

I don't want to talk to her about my feelings. I don't even know how to talk about my feelings. How do I get her to stop? I stare at the wall and don't answer, but she keeps talking. I don't really hear what she says, but I know she keeps going on and on. Wanna's voice is like a bee buzzing in my ear. I want to smack it away.

21

Dear Penny,

Ok. I will admit this to you and to nobody else…I was kind of excited when I found out that I was going to be adopted. I would have a family, and I wouldn't be on my own anymore. Remember the TV in the orphanage? Well, I spent a lot of time watching it. I watched movies about Americans. They were always rich. They wore fancy clothes, swam in their house pools, and went to restaurants all the time. You know what? It is not like that here. I don't have a pool and my parents don't wear fancy clothes. Sometimes we do go to restaurants.

The thing is, I still feel like I don't have a family.

22

Dear Penny,

Sometimes Wanna smells really good. She smells like sweet peaches and lemons. Don't tell her I told you so.

23

Dear Penny,

I was just thinking about the food in the hotels in China. It was really good. When I was adopted, the first gigantic hotel we stayed in had the best food in the world. The hotel restaurant had table after table covered with food. There was so much food. I couldn't believe it. I ate more than I ever ate in my whole life. I thought for sure that my new family was rich.

But there isn't food like that here in America. It was only like that in hotels in China.

The last big hotel we stayed at in China gave me a gift. It was two dolls in a small box. Inside was an American mom doll with a Chinese baby doll. The mom had long yellow hair. The mom doll held in her arms a little Chinese baby.

I don't know why the hotel would give me that gift. I was not like a baby doll.

I didn't like the mom doll, and I definitely didn't like the baby doll.

The hotel was filled with American parents adopting Chinese babies. The hotel food was very good and there was a lot of it. But I remember looking around the hotel restaurant, at all of the Chinese babies being held by American parents, and everything felt confusing. I felt like I wanted to start running.

But I didn't run. I ate instead.

I know that I pushed the hotel gift dolls away when Wanna showed them to me. I never saw the dolls again. I don't know what Wanna did with them, but I still remember how much I hated those dolls.

24

Dear Penny,

There is a fly in my room. It is dancing with the light above my bed. If it hits the light, will it burn? I hope it will hit the light. I hate bugs. In the summer bugs would come into the orphanage, and they would be everywhere. There were crawling bugs and flying bugs.

I don't know where the bugs came from, but they came with the heat. Once there was a girl who was sleeping, and a bug crawled into her ear. She screamed and cried for hours as the nannies poked different things into her ear to try to kill the bug and get it out.

The nannies got the bug out, but her ear was bloody when they were finished.

The bugs would die all at the same time, and it took days for us to sweep their dead bodies into big piles and sweep them out.

25

Dear Penny,

It is hard to keep the sand off you and me. I go to the lake with Wanna and Ellie, and I get dirty sometimes. I try not to play, but Ellie keeps making me play in the sand. I don't like to play in the sand because I am not under the beach umbrella when I play. I am in the sun. My sister Ellie has dark skin, and I want to keep my skin white. My skin is white like the pages of your paper. I don't want my skin to get darker. In China, the most beautiful people have white skin like me. Ellie's skin is too dark. Wanna puts sun lotion on Ellie, but she doesn't care if her skin gets darker. Wanna puts lotion on me too, but I don't trust the lotion. I don't think that Wanna cares about Ellie's skin. She says that my sister's skin is beautiful. In China, the whiter the skin, the better. I am proud that I am whiter than my sister. I don't want to be dark like Ellie.

26

Dear Penny,

I do like my sister Ellie's hair. It is long and shines in the sun. My hair is short. The orphanage always cut my hair short. I remember when they would cut it. I remember the big scissors with the black handle. I would put my hands over my face so they didn't see my tears. Who wants short hair like a boy? I didn't. But the nannies kept cutting it. There were also bugs in the orphanage that lived in people's hair. Everyone had their hair cut short so that the bugs didn't get in and start eating at your head.

I like Ellie's hair. I wish my hair were long and shiny. Wanna keeps cutting it, and I don't know how to tell her to stop. I don't cry about it anymore, but I wish I could tell her to stop.

27

Dear Penny,

My world has changed colors so fast and it scares me. The white walls in the orphanage to the bright rainbow colors in the cities of China. Now, in America, my life is filled with blue and green. The green trees are everywhere, and the blue lake looks at me every day.

28

Dear Penny,

I know you already know this about me. I steal things. You have seen me do it, but maybe you didn't know it was called stealing. In China I stole little things. They were little things that nobody even cared about...except here Wanna cares. She cares and she needs me to talk about it. I wish she would just hit me and get it over with. But Wanna won't hit me, even though I try hard to get her to. She keeps talking. Buzz, buzz. I am not talking to Wanna about why I steal things. I just like to do it. There is nothing to talk about.

29

Dear Penny,

Daddy is an architect. That is his job. It means that he designs houses. He doesn't build the houses, he just draws them on his computer. The people who buy the houses that he draws must be rich. The houses are very big and many have pools.

I like to sit on the floor next to his desk chair and watch him work. It is amazing to see how he does it. I think he must be very smart. Ellie watches with me sometimes, but it is hard for her to sit still and be quiet. Daddy needs to concentrate, and Ellie is always asking a thousand questions.

It is strange that Daddy designs new houses, and we live in such an old one. We don't have a pool either.

30

Dear Penny,

Jazz knows my name. When we go to the ice cream parlor, she says—

Hey, An-Ya, what's up?

I say hi and that is how the conversation ends. Jazz is much older and prettier and has so many friends. It always surprises me that she knows my name.

31

Dear Penny,

Forget what I said about Wanna smelling good. Her feet smell like stinky fish.

Wanna pushed me today. It wasn't hard, but it was definitely a push. I stole her special necklace and she wanted it back. I don't usually steal big things, but I was so mad at her the other day. I knocked Ellie over because she was being annoying and I couldn't stand it anymore. Ellie won't get up like Abby used to. She stays on the ground and cries. Wanna told me to go to my room and stay there until she came up to talk. I could see the mad in Wanna's eyes. Instead of going to my room, I went to Wanna's room and took her necklace.

So today she figured out it was gone, and she pushed me and told me to go get it. I couldn't go get it, because I threw it away yesterday and the trash man took it. So I held on to you and stared at my bedroom door. I'll never tell her what happened to it.

32

Dear Penny,

I think Wanna is still mad about the necklace. She asked Daddy to take me and Ellie out for the day. Daddy is much more fun than Wanna. He doesn't have so many rules and he doesn't try to talk about my feelings. He is ok. Plus, he is really tall. At first I thought he was a little scary, but now I like standing next to him. I feel small next to Daddy. I like feeling small. When I stand next to Ellie, I feel too big.

The best part of being with Daddy is that nobody asks him if I am his daughter. His hair is mostly black like mine, and they don't notice as much.

The playground that Daddy took us to is fun. There are places to hide and a lot of slides. The slides are my favorite. It is hard to play with the other stuff when I am holding onto you.

33

Dear Penny,

The orphanage walls were white. An ugly dirty white. Most walls were stained. The bathrooms were terrible. Do you remember the smell? It was a terrible smell. One bathroom door was always broken. A child was always sitting on every toilet. Sometimes they would sit for too long and start to cry. I tried to tell the nannies when the children were finished on the toilet. The nannies were too busy to hear me. There were too many children in the bathroom. They sat waiting for too long.

There was one wall in the orphanage that wasn't white. It was painted with big animals. Usually I would sit in front of the painting. Abby would sit behind me, holding onto my shirt, and we would stare at the wall. I liked the paintings on the wall. I don't know who put them there. The animals were the same size as me.

I miss the animals on the wall. I talked to them about things, and I think they heard me. There was the rabbit, the turtle, the monkey, the butterfly, and the mouse. I don't know what they were all doing together. But they were happy animals and they were friends. I am sure about it. I looked at them for many days, and I know they were good friends. Abby liked the monkey. She would point to the monkey the most. I liked the butterfly because she would leave at night and visit the moon. I wanted to be the butterfly. I wanted to fly away.

34

Dear Penny,

It takes a long time to walk to the lake. We have to walk through the woods. The first time I walked through the woods, I was really scared. I didn't know if there would be snakes or big bugs or something terrible like that. There is a trail that we walk on, and I stay as close to the middle as I can. I don't like my legs to touch the leaves and plants on the sides. Birds fly from tree to tree and watch us walk. Squirrels run up and down the trees and make funny noises.

Half way to the lake we leave the trail, step onto a road, and walk across a bridge. The bridge is painted red. It has a top on it and goes over a little river. Wanna said it is called a covered bridge and that it is very old. She said it was built around the same time as our house. I wanted to ask why it has a roof, but I didn't. I don't mind the bridge, because on hot days it gives me a break from the sun.

Walking to the lake wouldn't be so bad if we didn't have to carry so much stuff. We take a big umbrella, lunch, inner tubes, buckets, and shovels and towels. I am always stuck with a lot to carry, plus I need to carry you. Ellie can barely carry one bucket without getting too tired.

35

Dear Penny,

I am not as hungry at night anymore. When I first came here, I thought I would die if I didn't eat something after bedtime. I was starving. Remember how scary it was coming down the stairs in the dark? I took you to find food, and we would sneak upstairs with all kinds of things. When Wanna found the food wrappers under my bed, she asked me to stop. She gave me a box with food in it to keep in my room. I didn't like the food in the box very much. So we kept coming downstairs in the dark. We needed to be brave, because this is a big old house and there might be ghosts. Anyway, I don't feel so hungry at night anymore. I'm not sure why.

36

Dear Penny,

When it is hot, and we are not at the lake, I like to sit under the big willow tree outside my house. Most trees aren't interesting, but the willow is different. Its branches reach down and touch the ground. I sit close to the tree's big trunk and read or write inside of you. Sometimes sunshine will peek through, but mostly it is dark and cool. When the wind blows, the leaves sing and sway. I feel safe next to the willow with its giant arms surrounding me. I think the willow likes me too.

37

Dear Penny,

Wanna says we are the same. Not on the outside but on the inside. She says children are like a map. Sometimes their map looks like their biological parents. Sometimes their map looks like their adoptive parents. She says our maps are different on the outside, but inside there are some things that are the same. Wanna told me she understands the pain, and the pain telling me to do bad things. She has pain from the past too. She told me it is not exactly the same, but if you look at our inside maps they are very similar. I don't know.

38

Dear Penny,

I think Jazz is having problems. I heard her talking to a girlfriend in the parlor today. Jazz seemed upset and she looked like she had been crying. It was hard to hear exactly what they were saying because they were whispering and Ellie was singing and slurping her ice cream.

Something about Jazz's parents fighting and her mom leaving.

I understand how she feels. Daddy and Wanna had a big fight the other night. I could hear them yelling downstairs. I couldn't hear what they were saying, but their voices were loud and angry. Even if I couldn't hear the words, I already know that they were fighting about me. I am sure they wish they didn't adopt me. I am sure things were perfect before I got here. Wanna hates me because I cause so many problems. Wanna will probably be leaving soon too.

39

Dear Penny,

Do you like sleeping in the bed? It is huge. Wanna told me it was called a full size bed. I am starting to like it. When I first came home, I thought it was too soft and too big. It felt much better to sleep on the floor. Now I am starting to like the softness of the bed. What do you think? It's like sleeping on a cloud. I like this pink blanket with the flowers. But it would be much prettier if the flowers were blue. That is my favorite color—blue. I really like the blue that is a little lighter than the sky. When I have my own house, I will paint the whole house that color. Wanna says she hopes that I will never have my own house and that I will stay with her forever.

40

Dear Penny,

There was a Nanny in the orphanage who was like an angel. Her hair flowed down her back like a black waterfall. I loved her. She was beautiful and kind to me. Nap time was hard, and she always patted me on the head and sang a Chinese children's song. She would sing until I slept. Her voice helped me rest. I didn't see her very much. I don't know why she didn't come more. I thought that maybe she loved me. One day, after thinking about it for a long time, I asked her to adopt me. She laughed at me and it hurt a lot. I didn't tell her it hurt. I told her it was no big deal. But it was a big deal. She said that she wasn't old enough and she wasn't married. So what? It would have been much easier if she would have taken me. I would have brushed her hair for her. She would have let my hair grow long like hers. I would have been good to her and helped her clean. Nobody would ask us if we were mother and daughter because we would look the same. It hurt me that she laughed.

41

Dear Penny,

Today was a bad day. Wanna ordered me a surprise present on the computer. It came today. It was a Chinese super hero movie. Wanna knows that I like super heroes. I was excited about it, but I didn't tell Wanna. We opened the box and Wanna put it in the player. Then she left to go do the dishes or something.

It started to play the movie and I sat close to the TV. For a minute I was ok. I listened and listened, and I didn't understand what they were saying. Then my head felt a sharp pain. It was like a pain that went straight from my heart to my brain. I started screaming. I couldn't stand the pain. I screamed and Wanna came running. She held me. I think I kicked her. I think I kicked Wanna, but she didn't stop holding me. She turned off the movie, and we sat for a long time as I screamed away the pain.

Now my plan is ruined. I was going to go back to China. How can I go back now? The language makes my head explode.

42

Dear Penny,

Wanna talked to me about why the Chinese movie made me so afraid. She said it was common for children, adopted from another country, to fear their birth language. Wanna said it was like I took the Chinese language and put it in the bad memory part of my brain. So when I hear Chinese, it might scare me and remind me of difficult things that happened to me in China. She said it wasn't my fault and we would work on it together. I never imagined that being adopted was going to mean so much work. I wish my brain would have asked my permission before it started moving things around.

43

Dear Penny,

Wanna bought me a baby bottle. I told you that she was crazy. She said maybe I needed to take care of the hurt baby in my heart. It is a blue bottle. Somehow she figured out my favorite color. Anyway, she filled it with warm milk and I sat on the sofa. She turned on the TV and placed a blanket on my lap. She asked me if wanted to be held when I drank from the bottle. I told her I was fine. Ellie has a bottle too. Hers is pink. That is her favorite color. Ellie lies on the floor to drink hers.

I wasn't so sure about the bottle. It felt strange when I put it in my mouth. I am glad nobody was looking. I never felt that kind of warm softness inside my mouth before. The feeling surprised me. At first it was hard to suck the milk out. After a few tries, I figured it out. The milk made me feel sleepy. It made me feel warm.

Maybe I will try it again. As long as nobody watches.

44

Dear Penny,

It is night. There is a storm and it is keeping me awake. The thunder sounds like a giant jumping on my house and the lightning makes my eyes hurt. The rain is heavy and hard. I am using my lamp, but I don't know how long it will work. Every few minutes it will stop working and the dark comes.

I can't stop thinking about the babies who disappeared from the orphanage. Sometimes there was a new baby who arrived in the orphanage, and I was always told not to touch them. Usually they were very small. They were so small that it was hard to tell that there was a baby under the blanket. Sometimes their heads were too big for their bodies and sometimes their top lip would be opened as big as the world.

I was told not to touch them because they were sick and they could make me sick too.

I wanted to touch them, but I was not brave enough. It didn't seem ok for them to lay alone. I know they needed to be held, but I was too afraid. They would stay for one day, or two, or a week, and then they would be gone when I woke up.

I would ask the nannies what happened to them. They always said that they were adopted. I don't think so. I think they left this world and were gone forever. They were too sick to be adopted. This much I know. Nobody would adopt a baby who was so small or so sick, and adoption didn't happen that fast. The nannies lied to me.

So I started naming the babies. I had a little piece of paper that I kept under my pillow. I started giving them names and writing their names on my paper. It was an old piece of yellow paper. The babies were never given a name. At first I would ask the nannies what their name was. They told me that they were too young for a name. Soon I learned that they would not be given a name because they weren't staying in this world long enough. It was my job to name them. I wrote their names on my old yellow paper so that they would be remembered. Names are important.

I left their names, written on my old paper, under my pillow in China. I forgot about the paper when my American family came. I left the paper behind. I don't remember their names anymore, but I remember all their faces. I hope they can forgive me for leaving their names behind.

The thunder stopped. Now I just hear the rain.

45

Dear Penny,

Wanna never asks if she can read you. I take you everywhere, and she never says anything about it. Ellie used to ask me all of the time if she could look inside you. She doesn't ask anymore. I told her *no* too many times. Ellie said that you were pretty. She asked Wanna if she could have a pretty book to carry too. Ellie said that she wanted to be just like me. Wanna bought her a pink diary with a lock on it.

She scribbles in it and says that there are secrets inside. Ellie shows me her scribbles and makes up stories to go with the scribbled lines. Usually the stories are about mermaids. They are kind of funny, and she talks on and on like she really wrote something.

Sometimes Ellie doesn't write stories in her book but says that she wrote a song. The song is always about me. She will sing to me—

An-Ya! An-Ya! You are the best big sister in the world! I love you An-Ya! I love you forever. An-Ya! I love you. I love you so much.

I don't know why she sings those things because they aren't true. I don't talk to her very much, and I just sit and stare at her when she talks to me. Maybe she thinks I am listening? Maybe she thinks I care?

46

Dear Penny,

My sister is happy all of the time. I mean all of the time. It makes me angry. What is she so happy about? I guess I would be happy too if I had long shiny hair and everyone told me how cute I was.

I know how to make Ellie unhappy and sometimes I try. Once I told her that Wanna was going to give her away just like her first mommy did. I told her that Wanna would send her back to China. She cried so hard that she threw up. Ellie didn't let go of Wanna for three days. Wanna had to carry Ellie everywhere, and when she wasn't carrying her, Ellie was holding on tight to Wanna's leg.

I felt bad after I said it, but I didn't say so. Ellie's brain doesn't remember China but maybe her heart does.

47

Dear Penny,

Today Wanna made our family wear the same color clothes and go have our picture taken. Me, Daddy, Ellie, and Wanna all wore a dark blue shirt and tan pants and skirts. Me and Daddy wore the pants. Ellie and Wanna wore the skirts.

We drove to a place that Wanna called the studio. She made it sound like some special place where something exciting was going to happen. There wasn't anything exciting about it, except for a man that was taking our picture and who talked with his hands more than with his mouth. It was hard to keep from laughing at him. The man, the photographer, was crazy, and he kept saying crazy things. He kept yelling—

Smile! Smile! Perfect! Wonderful! You all look like movie stars!

Ellie believed him and smiled like she was a real princess.

I hope I never have to do that again.

48

Dear Penny,

Wanna says that I have a gift with languages. She said that it is an incredible gift. She says that what I have learned, what I can write and speak in English, is amazing.

What Wanna doesn't know is that my English teacher in China was not as excellent as he thought he was. When I first heard English spoken by my new family, it sounded strange. My English teacher didn't say the words the same. When he said English words, they sounded different. It took some time for me to figure out the right way to say things in English. Maybe Wanna is right. It didn't take me long to understand English. It was easy for me. I could read and write in English before I left China. I practiced all day, every day.

Maybe I have a language gift. If I have a gift for learning a language, then I must have a gift for forgetting a language too.

49

Dear Penny,

In the orphanage I used to sing. Not to anybody special. I would just sing because I wanted to. But the children thought I was singing to them. So they would stop their playing and come sit next to me. The orphanage would be quiet and filled with only my voice. Everyone said that my singing voice was pretty. Even the nannies.

I can't sing in English. I don't know how to try. Maybe my voice can only sing in one language, and now that language is gone? I miss singing. When I would sing, everything would be ok. I didn't think about anything else. I sang for me and my voice would touch the sky.

50

Dear Penny,

It is night again. It is raining again. The rain is loud and heavy, and the streets are filled with rushing water. I have been thinking about running away. In my room is a large window. It is almost as big as me. The window is tall with many glass squares. The top is round. But I can't open it. It doesn't open and let the cool air in. There are other windows in my room, but they are high up and small. Daddy opens those when it is warm.

I placed my hands on the large window and I thought about how to get through. I could push. I could bang on the window. But how do I break the window without the window breaking me? I wanted to go somewhere else. Somewhere where they don't ask about my past, somewhere where they don't ask any questions. If I hit the window really hard, then I could get out. I am strong enough. Maybe I could jump out of the broken window without cutting myself too much. I'm not sure.

Even if I cut myself on the broken glass, would that be so bad? Maybe I would be free to run with my blood flowing like a river into the wet street. Maybe it would feel good. Maybe it might even feel great. I could run so fast, and my blood could leave a beautiful painting behind me. The rain would wash the pain away.

51

Dear Penny,

Last night I couldn't break the window. I didn't even try. I put my hands on the window and felt its coolness. When I took my hands away, it left a white shadow of my hands on the window. I sat under the window and cried until I couldn't breathe. I started choking and Wanna heard me.

She came into my room and sat behind me. I felt her hand touch my head, and her fingers began to run through my hair. She spoke in a soft voice and told me how sorry she was. I stopped choking, but my eyes were blurry, and I couldn't see through the tears that continued to fall. Wanna kept touching my hair. She pulled her fingers through each piece and worked out all the tiny knots. I couldn't see her finger nails, but I knew they were painted a shade of pink.

I asked her to go away. I told her I hated her and to go away.

She didn't leave. She kept working her fingers through my hair and whispered how much she loved me and how she wished she could take the pain and carry it for me. She asked me if I knew why I hated her so much.

I told her that I hated her for cutting my hair.

Can you believe that I said that?

She said we didn't have to cut it anymore. We didn't have to cut it ever again.

52

Dear Penny,

Tonight Wanna gave me her old robe. It is soft, thick, fuzzy, and white and smells like sweet peaches and lemons. She told me it was a lucky robe and to wrap myself in the robe if I feel scared. How can a robe be lucky? She said that whenever she felt sad or scared, she would wear the robe and it helped her feel better. I don't know. I brought it to my room, but I probably won't use it.

53

Dear Penny,

Do you think that I have brothers and other sisters in China? Do you think She kept them and just left me?

Wanna told me today about laws in China that say that most people can only have one child. There were too many people in China, so they started making laws to make sure that there would be enough food and jobs for everyone. Wanna said that the laws were written a long time before I was born and they are complicated. Families in China hope for a boy, because they will stay with the family and will take care of their parents when they get old. Girls will leave the family when they get married. If a family breaks the law and has another child, then they have to pay a lot of money to the government. Most families don't have the money to pay.

So maybe She left me because I was a girl. How could She do that because She was a girl once too? I can do anything a boy can do, and I am smarter than all of the boys that I know. She didn't give me a chance. She put me in the box without giving me a chance.

54

Dear Penny,

The bad dreams won't stop. I am afraid to go to sleep. Abby has been coming to me in my dreams. In my dream I return to the orphanage and Abby is outside. She is not supposed to be outside because her skin will hurt. I run to her and she smiles when she sees me. She stands up, and some of her skin is sick from being outside. Somehow she wandered outside and nobody noticed. Her legs have black spots, and I am scared that her skin will fall off her body.

She is so happy to see me that she doesn't care about her skin. Her smile is so big and her grey eyes sparkle with happy feelings. I am happy to see her too, and I let her grab onto my shirt and I walk with her to find the orphanage door.

But again, I can't find the door. I don't remember where it is.

When I turn around to check on Abby, I see that she is growing smaller. A little bit at a time, she is shrinking. I tell her not to worry, that I will find the door. I search and search. Every time I look at Abby, she is smaller.

And then she starts to disappear. She becomes like a cloud that I can't touch but I know is there. She is so tiny that she begins to float away. As she starts to fly off, like a weak balloon, I reach for her and she reaches for me. Her tiny arms reach out and she whispers my name—*An-Ya.*

I can't catch her. My hands go through her body and there is nothing to hold on to. I can't bring her down. I watch her float away and there is nothing that I can do.

After I woke up, I put Wanna's robe on. I feel a little better but not all the way. I am still scared.

55

Dear Penny,

Tonight Wanna tried to teach me and Ellie a song. It was a song about a rainbow. The song is boring. Wanna has a nice voice, but the song is for babies. It goes on and on about the different colors of the rainbow. I can sing about a rainbow too, over and over again. After Wanna sang the song, she asked if we could see the rainbow in our hearts. She asked if we could feel the rainbow. *Oh, yes*—said Ellie.

What? I can see the rainbow. Sure. I see it. Can I feel the rainbow too? No. I don't even understand what she is talking about.

56

Dear Penny,

We went to the parlor for ice cream after spending all day at the lake. I chose chocolate.

57

Dear Penny,

Sometimes I don't know what to write inside you. Should I write about then or now?

Some days it is difficult to imagine that I lived in China for so long. When I think about it, it feels like one long day. So many days were the same and they all blur together.

Life in America is quiet. It is a strange kind of quiet. There is noise, but it is not the same. In the orphanage it could get very loud with many children crying. Usually it was the new babies that cried a lot. If you live in the orphanage for long enough, then you learn to wait. It doesn't take long to learn that nobody will be coming for a long time. I would notice when a baby would give up. Some were stronger than others, and some of them lasted longer and fought harder. Some babies would give up quickly. It is like they knew, even though they were babies, that their lives would never be the same and it wasn't even worth it to try.

58

Dear Penny,

Older children did not go to the baby room in the orphanage. I was different because I took care of Abby. I didn't take great care of her, but they let me in anyway.

Abby was too old for the baby room. I don't know why she was still there. She was too old for a bottle. But that is what they gave me to feed her. She slept in a crib, and sometimes I would sleep next to her. I slept on the floor. Her crib looked like the other cribs that lined the baby room walls. It was a metal crib, and she would look at me through the metal bars. I tried not to worry about the other babies. There were too many, and I knew I couldn't do everything for everybody. So I just looked at Abby in between her gray metal bars.

At night Abby would peek through the metal bars and point to her nose. She wanted me to touch it. She was happy when I tapped her nose at night. If I reached up and touched her nose, then her legs would kick and her whole body would smile.

The problem was that she kept asking over and over. She would look at me through the bars and whisper my name too many times. Once I was so sick of it that I pinched her nose really hard and left a finger nail mark in her pale skin. She continued to peek at me through the bars with wet grey eyes. But she didn't ask again.

The next day she had a black spot from my pinch. The black spot lasted a long time.

59

Dear Penny,

The noises in America are quiet. In the morning there are birds that sing. Their songs remind me of when I used to sing in China. It must be nice to be a bird and sing all day. Some birds sing the same song, and some of the birds never seem to sing the same song twice.

I know the sounds of my family's feet. I can tell who is walking and where they are going. Ellie's feet are light and quick. Wanna's feet are slow and soft. Daddy's feet are the loudest.

Wanna likes to use her sewing machine in the morning. It makes a humming sound with clicks that change from slow to fast.

Daddy goes to work in the morning. I can hear him washing his face, the swish and spit when he brushes his teeth and the flush of the toilet.

Ellie likes to play Legos in the morning. I listen to her spill them all out of the bucket and begin to snap them together.

There is a flag pole outside my room. On windy days I hear the flapping of the flag and the tapping of metal. It is the only sound that is familiar from my old life. When I couldn't sleep in the orphanage, I would tap the metal leg on Abby's crib.

I don't make any sounds in the morning. I lie still and just listen.

60

Dear Penny,

There was a boy in the orphanage that I hated. He was missing a part of one arm. Beneath the elbow was nothing. The elbow was smooth and round. He was long and skinny and one of the meanest people I ever met.

One day Abby was missing. I couldn't find her anywhere. It was strange and I started to look all over. I asked the nannies where she was, and they didn't know and they definitely didn't care. They were too busy with the babies to worry about it.

I walked around the orphanage and went in every room. I even went into rooms that I knew I wasn't supposed to go into. I walked in circles, and she was nowhere to be found.

As I was walking up and down the halls, I heard the Mean Boy yelling. At first I couldn't tell where his voice was coming from. I opened doors and he wasn't in them. I knew that if I could find him, then I would find Abby. I don't know how I knew. I just knew.

Then I stopped in front of the cleaning closet, and his voice grew louder. He was in the closet. It was a large closet with shelves that went high to the ceiling. I stood very still and listened for a minute. He was shouting—

You are so ugly! You are gross! You are stupid! Your grey eyes are the eyes of the devil!

I wanted to walk away, but I couldn't. I opened the closet door.

He didn't even look at me. He kept doing what he was doing for who knows how long. Abby was on the floor. She curled her body into a ball and was not moving. She was still and silent. She only moved when his leg kicked hard into her back. His strong kick pushed Abby slowly around the closet.

I had tried fighting the boy before, and he was too strong. I tried fighting him enough times to know that it would be worse to try. The only thing to do was to lie down, hold Abby's back against my belly, and wrap my legs around her to block his kicks.

He kicked my back for a long time. It felt like a very long time. And then he left. My back hurt for many days. Abby took a long time to stand up straight again.

He was a Mean Boy. The meanest. I hate him and I will always hate him.

61

Dear Penny,

I went to the lake today. It was so hot that I had to go in the water or I would die. I promise that I kept my eyes on you the whole time I was in the water. I didn't put my head under. Not even once. I stood in the water and watched you. The water is blue and clear and cool.

It is still hot and I am tired.

62

Dear Penny,

I stole things from the nannies. I stole things that they didn't need. The nannies had an office in the orphanage. They kept their things in the office. There were desks and chairs, but I never saw them sitting in them.

Actually, the nannies never really used the office. There were too many other things to do. I was not allowed in there, but I went in anyway. I needed to be careful because if I was caught in the office, then I would be in big trouble. I never got caught. I knew when to go in and I was patient.

I stole candy. There were little yellow hard candies that were wrapped in red. I loved those candies. I wanted to hold them in my mouth forever. I couldn't do that because the nannies would see me. I needed to bite down and crunch and chew as fast as possible.

For some reason American families who adopted children in the orphanage would give the nannies perfume and lotion. The nannies had many desk drawers filled with different smelling bottles. One time I found a perfume that I needed to keep smelling. I took it. It smelled like cookies. It made me smile when I smelled it.

I put the perfume in my pocket and quickly carried it to the baby room. In the baby room there was a wall of closets. There were many doors and many shelves. Inside the closets was everything that a baby needs. There were blankets and bottles and medicines. I knew the closets that were never opened. I put the perfume in the back of a closet that was never used.

I couldn't put the perfume on me, or somebody would notice. But I smelled the bottle every day. Sometimes I would smell the bottle many times in one day.

I miss the smell.

The perfume was one of many little things that I tucked inside the baby room closets. I wonder if they will ever be found.

63

Dear Penny,

My birthday is coming soon. It is a pretend birthday. I don't know how old I am, and I don't have a birthday. Wanna told me that when we were found in the box, we were taken to the orphanage. A doctor in the orphanage guessed my age and my birthday. He guessed. He didn't know for sure. The doctor looked at me and decided how old I was.

I don't have a real birthday. My birthday is a guess day.

Wanna asked me what I wanted to do on my birthday, and I told her nothing. I don't want to do anything. I never did anything in China for my birthday. Why should I start now?

64

Dear Penny,

The nannies called Abby the ghost baby. They whispered it, but I still heard them. When Abby arrived in the orphanage, they were afraid of her. They were scared of her grey eyes and white hair, and they thought that she was bad luck. I think that is why they put me in charge of taking care of her. The Chinese are always talking about luck, good luck and bad luck. They definitely thought that Abby was bad luck. So they gave her to me. Did someone else take care of her after I left, or was she all alone?

65

Dear Penny,

It is not much fun to steal from Ellie. She doesn't care. The first few times I tried it, she didn't even notice. One time Wanna caught me stealing Ellie's stickers. I don't know how Wanna does it. I never got caught in the orphanage. Wanna told me to say I was sorry to Ellie. I did to get it over with. Ellie said—

That ok An-Ya. You can have them.

Ellie would care if I stole her pink stuffed kitty. She calls it Sweet Pea. I wouldn't want to steal it, because she sticks the kitty's ear in her mouth all of the time. Sweet Pea's ear is always wet with Ellie's spit. I wouldn't want to steal something so gross.

66

Dear Penny,

Ellie is always asking me to sing with her. She sings with Wanna all the time. They have special songs that they sing together. They swing their arms and spin around the house singing. It makes me crazy. I watch them, but I don't sing.

In the orphanage the nannies made me sing for special people who would visit the orphanage. I hated it. I liked to sing for me, and I didn't like to sing for other people.

I don't know who the special people were, but they must have been important. The men were always dressed in suits and the woman wore high heels and lots of makeup. When the special people came, the nannies acted different. They would pat my head and hold the babies with smiling eyes. And then they would always ask me to sing.

Sing, An-Ya, sing.

The nannies would shove me to the middle of the room, and everyone would stand around waiting for me to begin. One time I stood and stared at everyone and wondered what would happen if I didn't sing. The nannies were getting nervous that I was taking so long to start. They were getting angry. It wasn't worth a slap in the face, so I started to sing.

67

Dear Penny,

Today Wanna made us do an art project. We sat at the dining room table, and she put out paints and markers and all different colored paper. Then she asked me and Ellie to paint or draw what made us feel scared. Wanna made a painting too.

Ellie scribbled with the markers and made big dots with the paint. She said the scribbles were snakes and the dots were spiders.

Wanna is a good artist. She painted a red car that was broken into pieces like a puzzle.

I painted balloons. Lots of colorful balloons. I hate balloons.

Then she asked us if we wanted to talk about our artwork. I said no. Ellie said yes and went on and on about her art. What was the point?

I thought about asking Wanna about her car painting, but I decided not to.

68

Dear Penny,

The Mean Boy in the orphanage stole things too. Except he wasn't as smart as me, just stronger, and he got caught. If something was missing, then he was the first person that the nannies suspected.

There was one nanny who had a watch. The watch had a red strap, and the middle of the watch sparkled with tiny jewels. She loved that watch and looked at it all the time. She was so proud of that stupid watch.

One day I was walking down the orphanage hallway, and the watch was sitting in the middle of the floor. I couldn't believe it. The nanny had dropped her watch. There wasn't anyone but me in the hallway. I ran to the watch and picked it up and put it in my pocket. I knew what to do with it.

I needed to be patient, but I needed to hurry. The nanny would realize her watch was missing soon. I hoped for the Mean Boy's room to be empty. I got lucky. The big kids were all in the TV room. A lot of boys slept in the same room as the Mean Boy. But that day nobody was around. As fast as my feet could move, I crossed the Mean Boy's room to his bed and tucked the watch under his pillow.

Whatever happened to the Mean Boy must have been pretty awful. I saw the nanny drag him by his hair into the office and slam the door. I heard loud banging sounds. When he came out, he went to his room and sat on his bed. He stared at the wall the rest of the day.

He stopped doing anything at all. He didn't eat. He just stared at the wall. He wasn't his same mean self for a long time.

I didn't know it was going to be that bad.

Tomorrow is my birthday.

69

Dear Penny,

Now I am 12. I am almost a teenager, which is a good thing because it means I am closer to being able to have my own house and be by myself. The only good thing about the art work we did the other day was that Wanna knew not to buy me balloons.

Wanna and Ellie baked a chocolate cake with blue icing. Daddy put 12 candles on top and everyone sang the birthday song. I was supposed to make a wish when I blew out the candles, but I didn't know what to wish for. I couldn't think of anything. So I just blew them out to get it over with.

Then I had to open presents. Daddy gave me a watch that has a crystal in the middle. It looks fancy. Ellie gave me a necklace with a charm that says sisters. I won't be wearing it. Wanna gave me a new quilt for my bed that she sewed herself. It is made of all different blue colored fabric. Some blue fabric squares have pink flowers inside to match the pink blanket on my bed.

After I finished opening my presents, I asked if I could go to my room. Wanna looked upset, but she said that it was fine.

Do you think She is thinking about me today?

70

Dear Penny,

Wanna is crying. I am in my room, but I can hear her. It is a loud cry mixed with a yell and a little bit of choking. It is my fault that she is crying.

She came into my room after my birthday party and asked me if I was ok. I told her she wasn't my mother and I wanted to go back to China.

I don't know why I said that about wanting to go to China. What is there for me to go back to? Nobody wanted me there.

I wanted to tell Wanna that I wanted my real mother and I wanted to spend my birthday with Her. I didn't say those things, but I said enough to make Wanna cry.

I don't belong anywhere. I guess I never did. I probably never will.

71

Dear Penny,

I see dancers in my head when music is playing. They are beautiful dancers and wear beautiful costumes. The music decides how they dance and what color their costumes are. I've always been able to see them. As far back as I can remember.

In the orphanage, the Nanny that I loved, the one that I hoped would make me her daughter, would play the piano. She wasn't very good, but the children liked it. Maybe she was better and it was the piano's fault. It was a dirty old piano with most of the paint worn off.

When the Nanny played, I would lie on the floor and listen. I would watch the dancers in my head.

Wanna plays music all the time. Different music on different days. Sometimes she tells Ellie and me to sit on the floor and listen with her. Wanna says to feel the music and let the music take us wherever we want to go. Weird, I know.

I don't know what I feel or where I want to go, but I like to watch the dancers in my head.

72

Dear Penny,

Wanna doesn't let me help her clean the house. She says that cleaning the house is a mother's job. She tells me it is my job to play. I have to pick up my own messes, but I am not allowed to help clean.

In the orphanage it was a child's job to clean. My hands were rough and my nails broke off as soon as they started to grow. Now my hands are getting soft and smooth, and my nails are longer then they have ever been. It feels strange.

A few days after I came here, Wanna took me to the doctor. She showed the doctor my hands and seemed worried that something was wrong with me. The doctor asked Wanna what kind of soap I used in China and if I was I forced to clean. I didn't say anything. I just listened.

The truth is I didn't mind cleaning the orphanage. I scrubbed the floors and metal cribs. I washed clothes and dishes in a big red bucket. It was something to do and I was good at it.

I'm not good at playing. I am much better at cleaning.

73

Dear Penny,

The same red bucket that I washed clothes and dishes in was the one I used to wash myself. I was responsible for washing Abby too. She would giggle when I washed her tiny feet.

Now I don't wash with water from a bucket. I take a shower. The water comes out of this metal thing, and it is like standing in the rain. I used to hate it, I was scared of it, but now I like it. I like the feeling of standing in the rain.

74

Dear Penny,

Ellie likes to sit close to me. She sits next to me and tries to rub my arm. Sometimes I let her and sometimes I don't. It reminds me of Abby when she rubbed the hand of the blind boy.

The blind boy in the orphanage wouldn't open his eyes. I don't know what his eyeballs looked like because I never saw them. The other kids were scared of him, but not Abby. He would stand in a corner and rock back and forth. He spent all day standing there and swaying.

He would make a strange humming sound and move the fingers on his hands. Sometimes, if he was upset, the humming would get really loud. I would take Abby over to him, but I didn't get very close. Abby would walk to him and reach up and rub his hands, and then his humming would get quiet again. I don't know how she thought of it, but it helped him feel better. I wonder if she still does that.

75

Dear Penny,

There are sounds and smells that remind me of the orphanage. I never know when or where to expect them. If I hear those sounds or smell those smells, the faces of the orphanage children come back to me. I forget now what most of the children looked like. It makes me afraid to see their faces in my head. I don't know why it makes me so afraid.

76

Dear Penny,

My new family gives lots of little kisses. Every time we say hello and goodbye we get a kiss. There are times that we get kisses for no reason. The first time Wanna kissed me for no reason, I was surprised. I asked her what she was doing. Wanna held onto me, and her yellow hair mixed with my black. She told me that in that very minute, her heart was so filled with love that she couldn't help it. I was not comfortable.

In the orphanage I received my first kiss that I remember. It was from a boy who I didn't think knew my name. I knew who he was. He had a large dark red spot that covered half of his face. His hair was black like the night. His eyes were shiny and he was nice to all of the children. I think he was older than me, but we were about the same size.

One day he was standing across the room holding his purple backpack. He was leaving. He was going to be adopted. I watched him talk to the nannies and say his goodbyes. Then he turned and looked straight at me. I was sitting on the floor next to Abby. I looked at her to see if she knew why he was staring. She was too busy playing with her toes to notice.

He dropped his purple backpack to the floor and started walking toward me. I didn't know what to do. I looked around to see if there was somewhere else he was going, but there wasn't anybody but me. It seems like it took forever for him to walk to the other side of the room. He stared at me and smiled the whole time he was walking.

Then, there he was, right next to me. I think I said hello. He didn't say hello back, instead he said goodbye. He said—

Goodbye An-Ya.

He said my name, and then he bent down and kissed my cheek. It felt like my cheek became red like his.

Everyone in the room laughed. I didn't laugh. My first kiss and another goodbye all happened at the same time.

77

Dear Penny,

For a long time after I was adopted, I felt sick to my stomach. My body understood rice and noodles, but it didn't like anything else inside it. I know I told you that I ate a lot of food in China, after I was adopted, and I did. But it made me feel sick. It was so incredible to be able to eat it all, but I think I ate too much.

After I came here, I stopped eating. I couldn't do it anymore. I felt awful. Wanna must have been worried because she kept asking me if I was ok. Then, when I wouldn't answer, she started cooking different food. Her rice and noodles don't taste the same, but my stomach feels better now.

78

Dear Penny,

Ellie's kitty Sweet Pea is missing. I didn't do it. Really. I have no idea where the stupid kitty is. Wanna thinks I did it, and she yelled in my face to give it back. I could feel Wanna's spit on my face as her words flew out of her mouth. Ellie won't stop crying. Daddy is mad at me too.

I hate them all.

79

Dear Penny,

Sweet Pea is still missing, and Wanna stopped asking me about my feelings. She hasn't asked me anything about them all day. Not that I would have answered her anyway. But still. She gave up. I knew she would. I knew it all along.

80

Dear Penny,

I feel pain. I have pain in my shoulder and in my back. I am sure that there must be bruises, and I keep waiting for them to show up. There is nothing. No black and no blue. Just the pain inside. I don't know what is happening to me. The pain is very real, but I didn't fall down or get hurt. It is not my imagination. When I try to lift my arms up or even as I am writing in you, the pain is there. I want the pain to go away. Go away pain, and stop bothering me. Uh oh. I think I am going to throw up.

81

Dear Penny,

Last night Wanna heard me throwing up. She took me back to bed and rubbed my shoulders. I was so dizzy that I didn't care what she did. She says I have the flu. I need to stay in bed until it gets better.

How is it going to get better? I am hot and cold and my whole body hurts. I don't trust Wanna to make it better. I need to learn more about medicine so I can fix these things myself.

82

Dear Penny,

Wanna has come to check on me a thousand times. She brings me soup and juice and keeps saying—

Drink more, An-Ya, you need to drink more, An-Ya, drink.

She brings me a hot wash cloth when I am cold and a cold wash cloth when I am hot. Wanna wraps me in her white robe, and a few minutes later will take it off and place it next to my body. She keeps doing these things over and over again, because every few minutes, my body changes from sweating to shaking.

Wanna rubs my head and sings to me. She sings about rainbows and bridges and angels and stars. It reminds me of the Nanny who I loved. The Nanny who sang me lullabies in the orphanage. The language is different, but the sound is the same.

I am so tired that I can't see the dancers in my head when Wanna sings.

Sometimes Ellie comes in and reads me her diary and sometimes she sings too.

I am starting to feel less pain, but I am so tired.

83

Dear Penny,

Wanna asked me who Abby was. I was so surprised that I didn't say anything for a long time. It was very strange for Wanna to talk about Abby, to hear her say Abby's name out loud, and it was even stranger that I wanted to tell Wanna about Abby.

My temperature was really high last night, and I was burning alive with a fever. I was so hot. In my sickness, my hotness, Wanna said I cried for Abby many times. Wanna said that I cried Abby's name over and over again. Wanna knew that I needed Abby, but she didn't know who Abby was to find her and help me get better.

I don't remember saying anything about Abby. I only remember burning.

I told Wanna about Abby, not everything, but parts. Maybe I am still sick. I don't know why I was able to talk about her. All I know is that Wanna said she will try to find out if Abby is ok. Maybe soon I will know how Abby is doing. I told Wanna that Abby is the only child in the orphanage with grey eyes and white hair. Wanna said that it was lucky that Abby looked different, but did I know if Abby was her Chinese name? No, I said, I don't remember her Chinese name. Wanna said—

No worries, An-Ya. I will do my best to find your Abby.

84

Dear Penny,

Wanna found Sweet Pea. Ellie forgot that she was playing hide and seek with Sweet Pea, and she stuck Sweet Pea in the clothes dryer to hide. Wanna found her when she went to wash clothes today.

Everyone came into my room and said that they were sorry. Ellie cried and said—

I so sorry, An-Ya. You are good and I am bad.

Wanna and Daddy said they felt terrible for yelling at me. They asked me to please forgive them. I don't know. What is the point of telling the truth? If I lie, then I am in trouble. If I don't say anything, then I am in trouble. If I tell the truth, then I am in trouble too. At least they said that they were sorry. That's something, I guess. I've never said I am sorry to them.

85

Dear Penny,

Today I was feeling well enough to go to the parade in town. I am still tired, but the pain is gone.

I have never been to a parade before. The entire town was there. There were people as far as I could see up and down the street. We carried foldable chairs into town and sat in front of the ice cream parlor. It seemed like it took forever for the parade to start, and I was nervous because I didn't know what would happen exactly.

Wanna gave me a bag and told me that it was for the candy. Where the candy was going to come from, I didn't know. As soon as the parade started, I figured it out. There were big cars with decorations and people in costumes who threw candy into the street, and all the children would rush out to grab as much as possible.

I didn't run into the street because there was plenty of candy that landed next to my chair. Ellie danced around like a crazy person and grabbed much more candy than me. I didn't have the energy to run around for candy. There was also loud music and marching bands.

The Mean Boy in the orphanage would have been jealous that I saw a real marching band. He was the marching band leader in the orphanage. It was not very good, not at all, and the orphanage marching band costumes were all old and didn't fit anyone the right way. The costumes were supposed to be red, and maybe when they were brand new they were, but they had faded and turned an ugly pink.

The Mean Boy had a stick for a baton. He would smack the other band members if he felt that they weren't following directions or trying hard enough. All of their instruments didn't work and sounded terrible. The instruments that they had were not even real marching band instruments. I didn't see any guitars in the marching bands today. I definitely didn't see guitars that were missing half their strings. The orphanage band had hats with a dirty feather that stuck up at the top. It was hard to not laugh at them because they took their marching band so seriously. But when they performed, the nannies would clap and the Mean Boy thought that he was really something special. Abby would clap too. I guess she wasn't old enough to realize how stupid the whole thing was.

Jazz was in one of the marching bands today. I didn't know that she played an instrument. She plays the cymbals. The cymbals are these big round metal plates that you bang together, and they are really cool. Watching Jazz play in the marching band was the best part of the parade. Her costume was my favorite color—blue. The sides of her pants sparkled in the sun.

86

Dear Penny,

I started bleeding down there. I knew it was coming because I overheard the nannies in the orphanage talking about their monthly bleeding. I just didn't know there was going to be so much blood. Plus, my chest hurts and my stomach hurts and feels like it is filled with dirty water.

To make things even worse, I had a huge fight with Wanna. I got blood all over my underwear, pajamas, and bed sheets. I took everything into the bathroom and started washing it. I put new underwear on and stuffed some toilet paper in them to soak up the blood. Well, Wanna opened the bathroom door. She surprised me. I guess she saw that I didn't have sheets on my bed or something. I don't know how she knew exactly, but I knew I didn't want her in the bathroom with me. I screamed at her—

Get Out!

She wanted to help me. I kept screaming at her to get out and finally she did. She slammed the door and walked away. I need to go find some clean sheets.

87

Dear Penny,

Daddy came to my room tonight and sat on my bed. He said that
we needed to talk about what happened with Wanna and the blood.
He said that I need to share with Wanna and I needed to let her help
me. She wants to help me, and she wants to help my heart and body
feel better. He said that I can't keep everything inside anymore, and I
have to find a way to be brave and share my pain and share my hap-
piness and share with Wanna what I need. He was very upset and he
kept touching his black hair.

Then he told me about Wanna when she was a little girl. There were
parts of the story that I wanted to put my hands up over my ears and
not listen to anymore.

Daddy said that Wanna's parents, my grandparents, loved adventure. They loved to be free and travel and go anywhere at any time
that they wanted. Sometimes that meant that Wanna could not go
because she needed to go to school. So if Wanna's parents wanted to
travel, then they would leave Wanna with her uncle.

The problem was that the uncle was bad. He was not nice to Wanna,
and if he wasn't happy, then he would hit her. Wanna was very scared
of her uncle, but she was afraid to tell her parents. When Wanna's
parents would return from their adventures, they were extra happy
and were extra nice to Wanna. They would bring her gifts and tell
her all about where they went and what they did. Wanna loved to listen to their stories. They needed to travel and explore, or they would
be unhappy. So Wanna kept it to herself that her uncle hit her.

As Wanna grew older, it wasn't a problem as much anymore. She was able to find friends to stay with when her parents went on their adventures.

One day after her parents returned from an adventure, they came to pick Wanna up at a friend's house. They were so excited to see Wanna, and she was so happy to see them too. Wanna and her parents got in their car, and her father started driving them home. Wanna's father was laughing and talking about their travels, and Wanna's mother was digging through her bags and giving Wanna gifts from their trip. Everyone was so busy talking and laughing that Wanna's father did not stay on the right side of the road. He let the car turn just a little into the wrong lane. There was another car and it was going fast and it hit them.

Wanna and her parents were taken to the hospital. It was too late for Wanna's parents and they were gone. They died before the ambulance came. Wanna needed an operation to get the car parts out of her body. When she woke up, the doctors told her what happened. They told her that her parents were gone and that they needed to rearrange and take things out of her belly to save her life. Some things that the doctors took out would mean that Wanna could never carry a child inside her body. In one day Wanna lost her parents and lost the children that would never live inside of her.

It was on that day that Wanna decided that she would adopt her children. Daddy said that she never looked back. Her only memory is hidden in a scar that runs down her belly.

I'm tired. I need to sleep now. I will write about it more tomorrow.

88

Dear Penny,

Last night, after Daddy told me Wanna's story, I went to find her. Daddy told me I needed to go and talk to her.

I found her in the kitchen next to the fireplace. The room was dark except for the fireplace. Wanna's yellow hair looked orange next to the fire. She was very still and didn't move when I came into the room. She just stood there looking at the fire.

I said—*I'm sorry. I'm sorry about your uncle, and I am sorry about your parents.*

Wanna turned her eyes to look at me. Her eyes were filled with water. She didn't say anything, she just looked at me.

I whispered—*Can I see your belly?*

Wanna turned her body to me, lifted her shirt, and showed me her skin underneath. I walked closer to Wanna to get a better look. There was a raised line, which started under her bra and went all the way down her belly. At the bottom of the line was another line that went straight across her belly. The scar looked like an upside down *T*.

I reached out to touch it. When my finger touched Wanna, she jumped back a little. I looked into her eyes and she nodded that it was ok. So I reached out again and touched the scar from beginning to end. Wanna's skin was warm from the fire and the scar felt hot.

I said—*Does it hurt?*

She said—*Not anymore.*

I said—*I have my monthly bleeding.*

Wanna stood there with her scar still revealed to me, and she said—

I know. It is called your period.

Then she wrapped her arms around me, and her shirt draped over my head. My ear pressed into her skin, and I could hear her heart beating. She held on tight and we stood there like that for a minute. Wanna was holding on so tight that it seemed like I better hold on too, so I wrapped my arms around her waist and squeezed.

And then we both cried. For a long time we cried.

89

Dear Penny,

I asked Wanna if I could take my blue bottle and drink my milk next to the willow tree. Nobody can see me through the branches. It is warm and bright today but cool under the willow.

Last night I had a dream about the Mean Boy. It wasn't scary, it was just strange.

In my dream I found the Mean Boy sitting outside the orphanage. I didn't understand why he was there, because he was adopted a few months before me. Why would he come back?

I remember the day he was adopted, and I remember his new family. He was so proud of them. They were a big family with five children already. The Mean Boy was child number six. Two of his sisters were Chinese, and the three boys looked like the parents. The Mean

Boy walked around the orphanage and told his family about all his friends. Friends? The Mean Boy didn't have any real friends, just people who did what he said because they were scared of him. Behind his back children would make fun of him and make fun of his half arm. If the Mean Boy found out that someone was making fun of his arm, then that person would be covered with bruises.

The day that Mean Boy was adopted, his face was one big smile. He looked happy. But in my dream he was sad. He said that he came back to get his baton and marching band costume. *Why?*—I said.

The Mean Boy said that his new family didn't believe him when he told them that he was important at the orphanage, that he was a leader, that he could make people listen and listen good. He told me that his new family didn't give him the respect that he deserved. So he came back to get his things and to take them home to show his family.

I asked the Mean Boy if I could touch his arm. He wasn't mean anymore, just sad, so he said yes. It was smooth and felt hot. I asked him if it hurt. He said not on the outside, but on the inside. He asked me if I hurt on the outside or inside, which was a strange question because there is nothing wrong with me on the outside.

I don't remember what I told him.

90

Dear Penny,

I saw Jazz at the ice cream parlor today. She looked pretty. I think she was wearing more makeup today because she has a boyfriend. He comes in to see her at work all the time. His name is Lex, and he is definitely who I would pick for a boyfriend. Lex is tall and has dark hair like Daddy. He is very nice to Jazz and makes her laugh and smile. Even when Jazz is making my ice cream or talking to another costumer, she is always watching Lex. They say silly things to each other and whisper in each other's ear.

Daddy doesn't act that way with Wanna. He never makes Wanna laugh, and he definitely does not whisper sweet things in her ear. They are not talking very much, at least not as much as they used to. When Daddy and Wanna would walk to the lake, they used to hold hands. They don't anymore. Daddy is working in his office more than he used to, and I never see him except when it is time for dinner and sometimes not even then. Sometimes I don't see him until I am getting ready for bed.

I don't know exactly what is going on, but I am trying to figure it out. Ellie doesn't seem to notice that Daddy is not here very much. She is her happy, dancing, and singing self.

91

Dear Penny,

My body is growing, and my hair is growing too. I don't like that my body is growing so fast, but I am happy about my hair. I can pull my hair into a ponytail for the first time.

My orphanage clothes don't fit anymore. Wanna had to buy me new clothes. She didn't buy me dresses because she knows that I don't like them. I have pants now, which look like Jazz's pants, except my pants have blue jewel hearts.

The problem is that the more I grow, and with every day that passes by, I am further from the truth. As my body grows, the more I feel like I will never know the beginning of my story. If only I could go back in time and see Her face and listen to Her conversations with Him. What did they say to each other? How does a person decide to leave their baby and a book in the street under a gate? How is it possible that She could decide that plan was the best thing to do? It doesn't make sense to me and it probably never will. The bigger I get, the more confused I feel. Because now I know that thousands of mothers have made the same decision that She made. Ellie's mother left her too. Every single child that was in my orphanage and orphanages around the world had mothers that made the same decision. They left their children and never came back. They left their children forever, and they will never know what happened to all of us. How can that be?

92

Dear Penny,

Sometimes when I turn your pages, I think that I will see Her. I think that one of your white pages will become her mirror and her reflection will appear. I imagine her face staring at me and wonder what She will look like, if She will be smiling, if She will be crying, or if She will just stare at me with empty eyes and feel nothing.

93

Dear Penny,

Guess what? I am going to get a dog. Jazz has a dog, and now I am going to have one too. I see Jazz walking her dog to the lake sometimes. Her dog is big and brown and skinny. I think I want a smaller dog.

Wanna said that we will go to a place called the pound to get my dog. The animals that live at the pound don't have any families. Most of them were given up by a family that couldn't care for them. It is going to be hard to decide. I wonder how many dogs will be there?

I will be responsible for feeding the dog, taking it outside to go to the bathroom, and cleaning up the poop. The poop part will be gross, but I am ok about the other things.

Ellie wants a dog too, but Wanna says that she is not ready for such a big responsibility. Why does Wanna think that I am ready? It doesn't matter, really—but I wonder.

94

Dear Penny,

Wanna, Ellie, and I went to the pound. I needed to leave you in the car because I didn't want you to get dirty from all the dogs. You wouldn't believe how loud it was in there. I thought my ears would explode. Plus, it smelled awful. I didn't even want a dog because the smell was so terrible. Wanna told me to hold my nose and take a quick look at the dogs and don't worry about the smell. Well, that was hard to do because I thought I was going to throw up.

I held one hand on my nose and one hand on my belly and we walked into the dog rooms. All of the dogs were in cages, and we needed to look at them through a metal screen. They were barking and jumping and stinky, and I just wanted to get out of there. Then Wanna told me that each cage had a paper that told about each dog—how old they were, what kind of dog they were, when they came to the pound, if they liked kids, if they were sick, if they liked cats, and if they were a girl or boy dog.

After Wanna showed me the papers on the cage doors, I forgot about the smell. I read the paper about each dog and each of their stories. As I read, the dogs jumped up on the cage doors and spun around and were wild. I forgave the dogs for acting so wild and making my ears hurt, because I knew that they wanted me to take them home so they could get out of that awful place.

Wanna and Ellie tried to get me to take a gold furry puppy. They asked to hold him and pet him, and they thought he was perfect, but he wasn't perfect for me. I kept looking.

Finally, I saw a dog picture that I liked, but I couldn't see her in the cage. There were two dogs jumping up and down, and I couldn't find the one that I liked. Finally one of the other dogs moved out of the way, and there she was, in the back of the cage, curled up in a small ball. She seemed like she already gave up on looking for a home.

She was white and tiny. Her paper said that she was two years old, that she was shy, that she wasn't eating well—they didn't know what kind of dog she was for sure, and that she was found tied to the pound's front door.

I told Wanna that I found my dog. She said—

But, An-Ya, you didn't hold her yet or spend any time with her. Why don't you take her out and play with her and then make your decision?

I said—

I already decided. She is the one.

I'll tell you the rest of the story tomorrow. My dog needs to go to the bathroom.

95

Dear Penny,

So the pound man took the dog I picked out of the cage. The pound man was big, and his gigantic belly peeked out of his red shirt. He needed to fight off the two big dogs, who tried their very best to get out too. He was kicking the big dogs and yelling at them. I thought those dogs were going to bite off his belly button. He grabbed my dog while sticking his knees into the big dogs and threw her at me. I caught her and right away she fit perfect in my arms. She wasn't the prettiest dog, but she was quiet. Her ears looked like white bat ears and her eyes were big and black. Her white fur was dirty with brown paw marks from being stepped on by the other dogs in her cage.

Wanna and Ellie said that she looked like an angel. They petted her head and told her over and over how sweet she was. Wanna said that I should name her Angel, and I thought it was an ok name. But what I thought about most when I was holding her was how I could feel her bones. She was so thin that her bones stuck out and jabbed my arms.

I decided to name her Angel Bones.

I like the name. Wanna and Ellie think it is a little strange, but they are happy that I used Angel, so they didn't say much about it.

I wonder what her life was like for the first two years. Did she get lost? Did she run away? I don't think that it was a good life. Angel Bones seems scared that I will hit her. I have to watch where I put my hand when I pet her, because if I put my hand up high and come down, she hides her head. I guess it might take some time for her to trust me.

The good news for you is that I don't think she chews stuff. I will put you up on my dresser until we are totally sure that she won't tear your pages out.

96

Dear Penny,

Sometimes I feel angry. I know so many words in English. So many. But there are not enough words in the world that would help me to be able to say exactly how I feel. Why am I so angry? It is like there is a black spot in my heart that I can sometimes cover up but sometimes I can't. When I fail at covering it up, when I can't hide from the blackness, I feel alone, afraid and angry.

Holding Angel Bones and petting her until she falls asleep in my arms helps turn the black spot to gray, but the spot never goes totally away.

97

Dear Penny,

So many things happened today that I don't know where to start. First, I will tell you about the new neighbors. No, no, no—First I will tell you about Lex's brother. I was walking down the street with Angel Bones, and I ran into Jazz and Lex. They were with a boy that I never saw before. I found out that he was Lex's brother and his name is Levi. He is the same age as me but taller. Lex and Levi's parents are divorced. Levi decided to live with his dad in Arizona for a while, but changed his mind and now he is living here again. Anyway, they all talked to me like I was their friend. I just listened and said—

Nice to meet you.

Levi has dark brown hair that falls over his eyes a lot. When he talks, he sweeps his hand across his forehead and brushes his hair off of his face. His eyes are bright blue and when he looks at me, it makes my ears burn.

98

Dear Penny,

The other thing that happened yesterday was this girl who showed up at our house. I was standing in the kitchen and I heard Angel Bones begin to bark. If a stranger comes to the door, Angel Bones gets excited and has this big loud bark. I don't know how such a loud bark comes out of such a little dog. Anyway, I went to the door, and there was a girl my size with dark brown skin and lots of hair braids that were tied with green bows.

What's up?—She said

I said—*The sky.*

Daddy told me that joke, and this girl thought it was the funniest thing she ever heard. She laughed and laughed and said—

You must be An-Ya. I'm your new neighbor. My name is Sitka Bailey and I live down there.

She pointed down the hill toward the lake. I asked her how she knew my name, and she said that her family met Wanna at the market and Wanna told them that I would be thrilled to have a neighbor my own age.

What? Why would Wanna say that?

I asked the girl about her name...Sitka. What did it mean?

She said that her mommy gave birth to her under a gigantic tree that was called a Sitka spruce. Her Mommy wanted Sitka to grow up big and strong just like the beautiful tree.

I asked the girl what her mommy was doing giving birth to her under a big tree. She said her parents were out hiking and that was when she was born. She said that she was born a preemie and was small. *Preemie* was a new word to me. Sitka said preemie means born early. She said that her daddy and mommy were doctors, so it was no big deal. They knew what to do.

Sitka asked me what my name meant, and I told her. In Chinese the *An* means peaceful and the *Ya* means elegant.

I never told someone the meaning of my name before. My name means something.

Sitka said it was a cool name, and I told her that her name was interesting too. Oh, Sitka also really likes Angel Bones, and Angel Bones seems to like Sitka too.

99

Dear Penny,

Today Sitka came over and asked if I wanted to go for a walk. I asked Wanna and she said that it was fine as long as I took Ellie too. It didn't seem fair to me, but I wanted to get out of the house, so I took her.

Sitka changed her hair bows to red to match her shirt. I asked her if it hurt having her hair in all of those braids. She said it hurt when her mommy was braiding it, but after it was finished, it wasn't too bad. I told her that I was growing my hair out and maybe I would try braiding it when it got a little longer. She said she would teach me and that it was easy to do, but since I was Chinese and not African, I might look dumb with a lot of braids. I agreed. It would probably look dumb.

I told Sitka that people in China don't ever see people who look like her with such dark skin and that people in China like their skin really white. Sitka asked me if I thought the same thing—if I thought it was better to have really white skin. I lied and I said no.

It was hard to have a good conversation with Sitka since Ellie was constantly interrupting and Angel Bones was pulling me all over the place. I really need to teach Angel Bones how to walk on the leash better.

Sitka likes Ellie and holds her hand and gives her piggy back rides and tells her jokes. I don't know why she likes her so much, but Sitka makes me laugh too, so I will just deal with it. Everyone seems to like Sitka. I don't know what it is about her, but it is hard not to like her.

100

Dear Penny,

Today Daddy had a talk with me and Ellie. We sat on the sofa and he said that he had some bad news. He said that our family was having money problems. Daddy said that a lot of people were having money troubles in America and that meant that the beautiful houses he drew wouldn't be built. People didn't need him to draw houses because they couldn't afford to build the houses that he drew. He said that we would now need to save our money and we wouldn't have money for anything extra—like going to the ice cream parlor and stuff. He also said that sometimes money troubles make marriage trouble and that he and Wanna needed us to be good so that they could work on their marriage. I didn't know what he meant by being good, but I think he meant that I better not cause trouble because if I did, then our family would fall apart. I also don't know what Ellie thought of all of this stuff, but she did say—

Daddy, is that why you and Mommy don't hug and hold hands? Is it the money problems? I can help, Daddy. I have a piggy bank that almost full.

You can have all of it, Daddy, and we can make the money problems go away. Ok?

Daddy pulled Ellie onto his lap and told her what a good girl she was and thanked her for her offer. I didn't realize that Ellie even noticed that Wanna and Daddy stopped holding hands.

101

Dear Penny,

Today I was sitting under the willow tree and trying to teach Angel Bones how to sit. I heard someone calling my name and turned around to find Levi on a bike. He has this cool bike that is dark blue with yellow lightning bolts on the side. He asked me if I wanted to ride bikes with him, but I told him that I didn't have a bike to ride. So he parked his bike in our driveway and came over and sat next to me under the willow.

I was totally confused and didn't know what to say. Why would he want to spend time with me? I mean, any girl would be more interesting than me, and his face looks so soft and his blue eyes sparkle and well, why me?

He asked me what I was doing and I told him I was teaching Angel Bones to behave. Angel Bones was jumping all over him, and he said it was a good idea to teach her some manners. And then he asked if he could help me. So we tried over and over again to teach her, and finally, just when we were about to give up, she sat and stayed. Levi got really excited and gave me a high five—well, he had to explain the high five thing because I never did it before. He thought that was really funny that I didn't know how to high five, and I was totally embarrassed. Anyway, I will never forget his hand slapping my hand. Actually, even after I got how to high five, I pretended I still needed help just to feel his hand touch mine again.

102

Dear Penny,

Sitka came over to make cupcakes. I didn't know that she was coming. Wanna called and invited her and surprised me. I wish she would have asked me first. What if I didn't feel like making cupcakes? But it was too late, and Sitka showed up at our house ready to bake.

Wanna loves to cook and bake. Whenever she is in the kitchen, she looks happy. She always wears a yellow apron that matches her yellow hair, and as she measures, chops, and stirs, her cheeks get really pink.

Wanna gave us each one of her old aprons to wear. Of course, Ellie looked ridiculous wearing an apron that was bigger than her body. Sitka thought that Ellie looked cute and every time she looked at Ellie, she would giggle.

The worst part is that when Wanna cooks she sings. Everyone but me seems to think that this is wonderful. Sitka and Ellie got really into it. I just sat and cracked my eggs and watched them.

How can Sitka be so comfortable with people that she doesn't know?

We put rainbow colored frosting and sprinkles on the cupcakes when they were done baking. Everyone but me seemed to have a great time. At least the cupcakes tasted good.

103

Dear Penny,

Will the day ever come that I feel comfortable in this place with these people?

104

Dear Penny,

Wanna saw me teaching Angel Bones some more tricks and asked me how I trained her. I told Wanna that Levi helped me and she looked worried.

She said—

You mean Lex's brother?

And I said yes. She said that she didn't think he was a good person for me to be spending time with, and I asked her why.

She said—

He stole things. He went away for awhile.

What? So Lex and Jazz didn't tell me the truth about why he was away? I told Wanna the story that I heard about why Levi left, and she said it was partly correct—Levi was in Arizona and his dad does live in Arizona, but Levi wasn't living with his dad. He was living at a place to help children who have stolen or committed other kinds of crimes.

So I said to Wanna—

I have stolen things. Does that make me a not good person to spend time with too?

Wanna looked surprised and said—

Of course not. I didn't mean it that way. You are right. Maybe Levi was having a difficult time and made bad decisions because of it. Just be careful, An-Ya. I don't want you to get hurt.

So Levi stole things. I wish they would have told me the truth.

105

Dear Penny,

It is the middle of the night, but I want to write this down so I don't forget.

I was dreaming about Abby again. She was sitting on the floor of the orphanage and staring at the wall with the big animals painted on it. Big tears were rolling down her face as she pointed to each animal and quietly said their names in English—*turtle, monkey, butterfly, rabbit, mouse.* And then she would point to herself and shake her head and say—no name. Over and over she kept repeating the animal names and pointing to herself and saying—no name.

It was so sad to watch her and I couldn't speak to her. She couldn't see me. She couldn't see me standing there. I tried to touch her, but I felt nothing and she felt nothing in return.

No name.

And I woke up. I woke up and sat up straight in my bed.

I remembered her name. Just like that her Chinese name came to me as fast as it left me before.

I ran to Wanna and Daddy's room and pounded on their bedroom door. Wanna called out—

What is going on? Is everything ok?

I opened the door and walked through the dark room over to their bed. Both of them were starting to get out of bed, and both of them looked worried. I have never gone into their bedroom before, let alone in the middle of the night.

I walked around the bed to Wanna's side, and she stared at me trying to figure what in the world I was doing. I didn't even know myself what I was doing and how I ended up in their room.

I said—

I know her name. I remember her name.

Wanna said—

Whose name? Whose name do you remember?

And she reached out to me and pulled me close to her. Wanna's hands were warm, and she held onto my shoulders and stared into my eyes with concern.

I said—

Abby's name. I remember Abby's Chinese name.

Wanna pressed my shoulders and said—

Can you say it out loud? Say her name to me.

And I did.

Ye-Bi. Ye-Bi is her name. Yee-Bee.

Wanna whispered Ye-Bi's name and then asked me if I wanted to stay. I told her no, that I was going back to bed now. She lifted her warm hands from my shoulders and said—*goodnight.*

106

Dear Penny,

It was hot today, and Wanna decided to take me and Ellie to the lake. Angel Bones loves going to the lake and will let me carry her into the water when she gets too sandy. I splash the sand off, and she lies still in my arms while I do it and closes her eyes. I think she really likes it.

On the way to the lake, as we were crossing the covered bridge, Wanna spoke to me about Abby. She wanted me to know that she hadn't forgotten her promise to search for her and find out if she was ok. Wanna said that maybe it will help now that we know her Chinese name.

107

Dear Penny,

This was a bad, bad day that started out fine.

Wanna ordered a Chinese cookbook on the computer and it came in the mail today. She was excited to try some of the recipes, so she took

Ellie and me to the market next to the ice cream parlor. Even though the market is small, it carries food from a lot of different countries like India and Japan. There is a little section in the back of the market that is labeled—International Food.

While Wanna searched the International Food shelves, I looked inside the ice cream parlor. I saw Levi and Lex sitting on the red stools. They were laughing about something, and Jazz was holding her arms on her hips and frowning at them. I didn't want them to see me, so I went back in the market to find Wanna. But I guess they saw me anyhow, because before I knew it Levi was standing next to me.

He said—

Your hair is really shiny today.

I said—

Is that a bad thing?

He said—

No. Not at all. It is a really good thing.

And then he smiled that amazing smile that makes my ears burn. He asked me to come into the ice cream parlor, but I said no. I told him I needed to stay with Wanna and do some stuff at home. Luckily he didn't ask me what stuff. He told me that he would catch me later and said goodbye.

We left the market after Wanna found substitutes for the ingredients that the market didn't carry.

Later in the evening she began cooking. The house filled with incredible smells as Wanna heated up sesame seed oil. I stood next to her and mashed the ginger root. It seemed strange to me that the smell of Chinese food was unfamiliar. We didn't eat food like that in the orphanage. There was no soy sauce or snow peas.

During dinner Wanna told us all about the things she learned from her cookbook. She talked about the ingredients and a little bit about the history of Chinese cooking. It was all interesting and even Daddy asked a lot of questions—most of which Wanna didn't know the answers to yet. Wanna and Daddy seemed happy—it was the way they were looking at each other. I haven't seen them look at each other that way in a long time. Ellie slurped her noodles and kept saying—*yuummmm*. It really was delicious and I felt a little bit happy too.

I helped Wanna clean up, and she kissed me on the head. I smiled at her and she smiled an even bigger smile back.

Everything was good and then I went to take a shower.

I am too upset to write about it now. Maybe tomorrow.

108

Dear Penny,

Last night I went to take a shower. It felt good to stand under the warm spray of water, and I stayed in the shower for a long time. I like the smell of the shampoo Wanna gave me to use. It is a melon scent, and the smell stays in my hair for a long time after it dries. I was having such a good time in the shower that I started humming a little and was surprised by how nice my voice sounded inside the bathtub.

After my shower I wrapped a towel around my body and one towel around my hair and headed back to my room to get my pajamas.

When I got to my bedroom door, I saw Ellie's back and she was sitting on my floor. I asked her what she was doing, and she didn't answer me. She was holding a rag, and I couldn't tell what was under the rag. I asked her what was under the rag and she wouldn't answer. She looked up at me and started to cry.

I started to get mad and said—

What is under the rag, Ellie? Lift up the stupid rag and show me.

She wouldn't move. Ellie just held her hands over the rag and stared at me, crying.

Finally I yanked the rag out of her hands.

And I found you.

There you were with grape juice on your page from Ellie's sippy cup.

Before I knew what happened, my hand flew across Ellie's cheek and hit her hard. She screamed so loud that Wanna was there before I could blink. I didn't realize that, as I was slapping Ellie, my towel fell off, and I was standing there naked. You were on the ground. You were open and stained. Ellie kept screaming.

Ellie's cheek was bright red, and Wanna scooped her up and took her away, leaving me standing naked and alone.

I picked up my towel and wrapped it around me. I picked you up and crawled into bed and hid under the covers. I didn't know if I wanted Wanna to come back for me or if I wanted to be left alone forever.

109

Dear Penny,

Why did She leave me? Why did She leave me? Why did She leave me? Why did She leave me? Why did She leave me? Why did She leave me? Why did She leave me? Why did She leave me? Why did She leave me? Why did She leave me? Why did She leave me? Why did She leave me? Why did She leave me? Why did She leave me?

Why.

I want to crawl back into Her belly and start over again.

110

Dear Penny,

Ellie's cheek looks purple now. I can't stand looking at her. She is afraid of me now. When I come into the same room as her, she runs and hides between Wanna's legs.

Wanna isn't speaking to me. I keep waiting for her to ask me to talk or to say sorry to Ellie or say something, anything. Wanna won't even look at me. Daddy hasn't been home. He has been working really late.

Just when I was starting to feel comfortable, when I was starting to feel like I might fit in here—I messed it all up. I let myself down, I let you down by not keeping you safe, and I let my family down. I'm sure I let Her down too. I mean, she didn't put me in the box expecting me to grow up smacking people. Right?

111

Dear Penny,

Sitka came over and wanted to play with me. I asked Wanna if it was ok and she waved her hand at me and said—*Go.*

So I put Angel Bones on a leash and left.

Sitka wanted to know why Wanna was acting weird, and I told her that Wanna was mad at me for smacking Ellie in the face. Sitka asked me why I would do something so mean, and I told her that Ellie stained you. I told her about us being found in the box together.

She didn't really get it, why you were so important. She said that no book was more important than a sister. Sitka said that she wished that she had a sister and especially wished that she had a sister as sweet as Ellie. I think she was mad at me too. She told me that I needed to say sorry and be extra nice to Ellie to make up for it. I don't think that saying sorry will fix things. I don't think I am worth forgiving.

Sitka let it go and we played. She wanted to hunt bugs, but I thought that was too gross and plus we didn't have anything to put the bugs in. So instead we played that we were superheroes. I had the super power of seeing through things. I could see through houses, trees, even people. Sitka wanted the super power of reading people's minds. Angel Bones had super sniffing powers. We are probably too old to be playing superheroes, but Sitka didn't care. She seemed like she was having fun and was being really funny. When someone walked by, she would tell me what he was thinking and it was hard not to laugh. She said one man was thinking that he wished that he could run down the street in his underwear.

112

Dear Penny,

I did what Sitka told me to do. I said I was sorry. It took some time to get the words out. I sat in my room and thought about it and then would go and find Ellie and she would hide. So I went back to my room and sat on my bed and thought some more until I was ready to try again. It took several tries before I finally went back and the words came out.

Ellie was sitting on a kitchen stool and watching Wanna cut celery up. They were making tuna fish sandwiches together. When Ellie saw me, she jumped off of the stool and stood next to Wanna. It was hard to look at her with her cheek still marked by my hand. I walked up to Ellie and bent down and said—

I am sorry, Ellie. I know you are scared of me, but I didn't mean to hurt you. It's just that my book is really important to me. I shouldn't have hit you, and I won't do it again.

The words came out exactly the way I had practiced them. Ellie stared at me and I waited for her to say something. Wanna didn't say anything and kept cutting the celery without looking up.

Finally Ellie stepped away from Wanna—and took my hand and kissed it.

And then she stepped back to Wanna's side. I said—

Thanks Ellie.

…and walked back to my room. I don't know how she forgives so easily.

113

Dear Penny,

Sitka went with us to the lake. Her parents work a lot at the hospital, and Wanna told Mrs. Bailey that she would watch Sitka for the day. Wanna still isn't talking to me very much. Ellie wanted to hold Sitka's hand while we walked to the lake.

It was warm enough to stand in the lake for a few minutes at a time. I couldn't stay in any longer without getting goose bumps.

There were two girls at the lake who I never saw before. They were around my age and were wearing matching rainbow bikinis. For some reason they came up to Sitka and me and started talking and saying—

So do you live around here, because if you do, you must be pretty bored and thank God we won't be staying long and where did you get that bathing suit and why are your dog's ears so pointy?

Then one of the bikini girls said, as she pointed to Ellie—

Is that your real sister?

And I said yes.

And then she said—

So where's your real mother?

And I pointed to Wanna. And she said—

So is your dad Japanese?

And Sitka said—

She is Chinese not Japanese, and no, her father is not either one.

And the bikini girl said—

Well, then, that is not your real mother because she is white.

And Sitka said—

Where is your real mother?

And the bikini girl pointed to a woman lying on a big yellow beach towel.

So Sitka said—

That can't be your real mother because she has brown hair and your hair is blonde.

And the other bikini girl said—

Well, they are both white. Duh.

And Sitka said—

So what do you want—a matching whiteness award? Or maybe she *is your mother because she's white...*

And Sitka pointed to Angel Bones.

The bikini girls told us that we were stupid and walked away. I was laughing so hard that I felt some pee come out and went back into the lake to wash it off of my suit.

114

Dear Penny,

Today started out pretty boring. I took Angel Bones outside to play, but she lay down in the grass and fell asleep. So I lay down next to her and looked at the sky. The clouds were huge and puffy and the sky was a bright blue. I played a game that Ellie plays all the time and tried to find animal clouds. I found a duck with a big beak and a horse that was missing a leg and a tail. And then I heard a voice above my head—

Hi An-Ya.

I looked up and saw an upside down version of Levi standing over me. I don't know how he does it, but he rides up on that lightning bolt bike and I don't hear a thing.

He said—

So watcha doing?

And I said—

Nothing really. Just thinking.

I wasn't about to tell him I was playing a silly kid's game with myself.

He said—

Sometimes I lie in the grass and try to find clouds that look like things. I found one that looked like a motorcycle once. It was pretty cool. So can I lie down and think with you?

Before I answered him, he went ahead and lay next to me. I didn't look at him. I kept staring at the sky and started to pull up pieces of grass and slowly ripped them apart. I could feel an ant walking on my leg, but I didn't want to sit up and brush it off. I didn't want to move.

Levi said—

Is something wrong?

And I said—

You lied to me.

He said—

What are you talking about?

And I said—

The stealing. You lied about why you were gone.

And he said—

Oh.

I said—

I could have understood. You didn't have to lie.

I wanted to tell him that I stole stuff too. I wanted to tell him that I understood. But I didn't.

He said—

Lex and Jazz think that you are really cute.

I said—

Oh?

Levi said—

But I don't think that you are cute.

I wanted the ground to open up under me and swallow me and cover me over with dirt forever.

Then Levi said—

I don't think you are cute. That is not a good word for you. You are pretty. Not cute. Plus, you are not like other girls who giggle when they talk to me and act all weird.

I didn't know what to say. I couldn't believe that Levi, the boy whose smile made my ears burn, thought that I was pretty.

I said—

I have stolen things before.

It came out of me even when I was trying so hard to hold it in. I didn't look at him after I said that because I wasn't sure if he even heard me.

What happened next was even harder to believe.

He grabbed my hand. Well, not really grabbed, but slid my hand off of my chest and rested it with his in the grass. His skin felt rough and it made mine feel smooth. He rubbed my palm with his thumb, told me he was sorry he lied, and then he pointed to the sky and showed me a cloud butterfly.

Angel Bones slept through the whole thing.

115

Dear Penny,

Tomorrow Wanna is taking Ellie and me to an Asian food market. It is a one hour drive to get there. I will need to be given car sick medicine because I get very sick. Driving around China was horrible.

I can't even count how many times I threw up. The airplane was awful too.

Wanna said maybe going to the market would be a good change to be around people who look like me and Ellie. Wanna thought that maybe I might recognize some food that was familiar and we could buy it and bring it home. I told her that mostly we ate rice in the orphanage. The rice had vegetables on top and sometimes a little meat. Sometimes we had a clear soup. A nanny would watch the kids to make sure that they ate all of their food. If we weren't eating fast enough, then she would give us an angry look and point to our food.

Anyway, I don't expect to recognize any food but rice, and I am worried about being around a lot of Asian people.

116

Dear Penny,

The drive to the Asian Market was terrible. It felt like it took forever to get there. At one point we stopped at a red light. I looked into the car stopped next to us and saw a little boy who was my age. His head was pressed against the window, and he was staring up at the sky. Next to him was the man driving, and he looked like the little boy— just bigger. The man was screaming at the boy. He was angry and kept hitting the boy in the shoulder. The boy just kept looking up to the sky. What if someone like that man would have adopted me?

Right as the light turned green, the boy looked straight at me. His eyes were empty. I don't know what he saw in my eyes.

The Asian market was much bigger than I thought it would be. It had Japanese food, Korean food, Chinese food, and all different Asian countries that I never heard of before.

And there were a lot of Asian people. It was easier than I thought it would be. People were speaking a lot of different Asian languages. I couldn't understand what anyone was saying and I wasn't too bothered by that. That was good because I was worried about how I would feel about the talking. What did bother me is that it was so obvious that Ellie and I didn't match Wanna. If I walked in there without Wanna, then it would be so much easier. I wish Wanna would have stayed in the car and handed me the money to buy stuff. I felt like people stared at us because we don't match. Lots of people asked us where we were from and where were we born. People congratulated Wanna, and Wanna said yes, she was very lucky to have us as her children. It was so uncomfortable. Some people didn't say anything to us, but just gave us the thumbs up sign. That was weird because after I was adopted, people did that to us in China too.

We bought some food to try for cooking another Chinese meal. People looked happy to help us.

There was one great thing that happened, and you won't even believe it...

Remember the Nanny that I loved? Sometimes she would sneak me this little jelly candy in a tiny cup. It came in different colors and flavors. I couldn't believe it—the Asian market had my Nanny's special candy.

When I saw it, I started jumping up and down. I couldn't control myself.

Wanna and Ellie jumped up and down with me—I guess they had never seen me so happy before and it made them really excited. Wanna bought a huge bag of jelly candy in a cup. I said thank you.

Ellie begged Wanna to buy her all of the toy things they had in the gift section. I liked that stuff too, but I stayed quiet and held my candy bag.

117

Dear Penny,

Sitka came with us to the lake again today. I gave Sitka one of my Chinese jelly candies. She said it was great and called the candy *very cool*.

It wasn't hot enough to swim but warm enough to wear shorts. I have these new blue shorts with big white polka dots. Sitka said that she loved my shorts and was going to ask her parents to get her a pair too so we could match. I asked her why she wanted to do that, and she said it was some kind of friendship thing that girls do—they wear matching clothes to show that they are best friends. I didn't know that we were best friends, but I am ok with it. I guess that means that she has forgiven me for hitting Ellie.

We helped Ellie make a sand castle and then we took Angel Bones for a walk on the beach. She is doing really well now on the leash. I have been working with her. She doesn't even really need the leash anymore. She will walk with me everywhere I go, and she doesn't ever try to run away. But the lake beach has rules, and one of them is that your dog needs to be on a leash.

On our walk I told Sitka about what happened with Levi. She couldn't believe it and kept saying—

No way! No way! Get out!

She told me I needed to be careful with boys and I asked her why. She said because—

They will play you.

I asked her what she meant by 'play me' and she said—

You know, An-Ya, they will play with your emotions.

I asked Sitka why she thought Levi would *play* me, and she said because he might want to touch my boobs. I told her she was crazy because I barely even have boobs for him to touch.

118

Dear Penny,

Ellie's birthday is soon and she is really excited about it. Of course, she wants balloons. She said she wanted them to all be pink, except for one that should be yellow and one that should be blue. Wanna asked her why she chose those colors, and she said that the pink ones were for her, the blue one was for me, and the yellow one was so the party would be sunny.

What is so great about balloons anyway? I don't get it.

In the orphanage everybody liked balloons. The kids made such a big deal about them—even Abby. They would blow them up and toss them around and then untie them and take the air out and use them all over again until finally they would tear or pop.

The Mean Boy was always trying to break other people's balloons with his marching band stick. One time he popped Abby's balloon, and she cried for the longest time. She didn't usually cry very much, hardly ever, but she cried for hours over that stupid balloon.

119

Dear Penny,

It is late and I want to go to sleep, but my brain can't get Levi's face out of my head. Do you think that he is thinking about me? Probably not. He probably didn't mean anything by holding my hand. It was probably no big deal to him. I wish it wasn't such a big deal to me.

Sitka asked me today if Levi was my boyfriend. I said no. She told me that I was lying and that I shouldn't lie to my best friend. So I admitted that I hoped that he would be my boyfriend someday, but really I didn't have any idea what we were or if there even was a 'we'.

Honestly, I don't even know what happens when you have a boyfriend. I asked Sitka what boyfriends and girlfriends do and she said write love letters and poems to each other and stuff. Maybe I should start practicing writing poetry? Wanna has some poetry books. I guess I could study those.

120

Dear Penny,

I have news, but it is not all good.

Wanna came into my room today. I was trying to braid my hair. My hair is longer, but I can't braid it yet without the braid sticking straight out from my head.

Wanna asked me to sit down on my bed with her and have a talk.

I didn't know what she wanted to talk about. She was holding a map and a piece of paper.

She said—

I have news for you about Abby…about Ye- Bi.

I wanted to be excited, but Wanna didn't look excited. She looked concerned.

I said—

What is wrong? Did something happen to her?

Wanna said—

No, nothing happened to her. She is fine, An-Ya. She is completely fine.

I said—

Then what is it? What are you looking at me like that?

And she said—

An-Ya, I really wanted finding Abby to be a wonderful experience for you, and I tried to make that happen. It didn't turn out exactly as I had hoped...but, I did find her and she is ok. She was adopted by a family in Canada.

And then Wanna showed me the map of North America. She pointed to where we are on the map and where Abby was in Canada. Abby is above us. Up higher. I stared at the map and waited for Wanna to tell me the part that went wrong.

It felt like we stared at the map for a long time in silence. When Wanna finally spoke again, it surprised me.

She said—

I found the family's address and wrote them a letter and sent them your picture. How I found them is a little complicated—but I did find them and wrote to them right away. Today I received a letter back.

Wanna looked at me and looked back at the paper she was holding. I couldn't imagine what the problem could be?

She said—

Her parents let me know that Abby is well. Her name is no longer Ye-Bi. They didn't say what her new name was, only that she has one. They said that she was happy now, but she was very unhappy when she was first adopted. The parents are very concerned about bringing back bad memories.

They showed Abby your picture.

Wanna stopped talking and looked at me with watery eyes. I was afraid to listen to what she said next. I put my head down so I didn't have to look at Wanna.

And then she continued—

An-Ya, when Abby saw your photos, she began to cry. Her parents couldn't soothe her. She rubbed the picture with her hands and was sad for a very long time. Her parents feel that it would be best for Abby if we no longer contact them. They want to put Abby's past behind her, and they feel that continued contact will only upset her.

Wanna put her hand on my shoulder, and I looked up and said—

How can they do that? How can they pretend that her life in China didn't exist? How can they erase me?

Wanna rubbed my shoulder and said she was so sorry over and over again. I wasn't sure if her hand was shaking or my shoulder was shaking, but I couldn't make my body still.

121

Dear Penny,

I forgot to tell you that after Wanna told me about Abby, she left my room and told me to wait just a minute for her to return. I sat on my bed and continued to shake even after she lifted her hand from my shoulder. I waited, but I didn't know what I was waiting for. When she returned, she handed me a photo.

It was Abby.

Her parents were erasing me from Abby's life, but they decided to send me a photo. None of it made sense.

Abby was riding a purple tricycle. She was wearing sunglasses and smiling. She was wearing a dress. It was so strange to see her in a dress. I never saw her in a dress in China. The dress was decorated in ladybugs. She was wearing a big hat that matched the dress and it was also decorated with ladybugs. Even her sandals had big ladybugs on the top.

I asked Wanna—

Why is she decorated in ladybug clothes?

Wanna told me that some parents who adopt from China believe ladybugs are good luck. Parents believe when they see a ladybug that it will bring them closer to their children—that finding their child or going through adopting them will be faster if they see a ladybug.

I asked Wanna why. What did ladybugs have to do with lucky adoptions?

Wanna said—

Now that I think about it…I have no idea.

I said—

That is the most stupid thing that I ever heard of. That is so stupid.

Wanna said—

I understand how you feel, but please don't say the word stupid. *Think of another word.*

I said—

There is no other word for thinking ladybugs and adoptions go together. It is totally stupid.

And Wanna said—

Well, I guess you are right. Maybe it is stupid and there is no other word.

I said—

To dress a child up in adoption ladybugs is even more stupid.

Wanna said—

They are just trying to show how happy they are to have Abby home now.

I said—

Did you do that? Dress Ellie in ladybug clothes?

Wanna looked embarrassed but admitted that she bought a lady-bug T-shirt for Ellie when they were in China. She told me that she would make sure to never buy me any clothes with ladybugs on them. I told her that I would never forgive her if she did.

122

Dear Penny,

I can't stop looking at Abby's photo.

I wish she wasn't wearing those sunglasses. I know that she is smil-ing, but I can't tell if her eyes are smiling too. If I could see her eyes, then I could tell if she was really happy and not just pretending.

When I look at her photo, I lie on my back and hold her picture over my head. I need to look at it that way because if I am looking down at her, instead of up, my tears might drop onto the picture and ruin it.

So I look at it when I am lying in bed on my back and hold her picture over my head. That way the tears fall down the sides of my face and soak into my pillow. Her photo is safe.

If her parents didn't erase me from her life, then maybe I could have taught them how to help Abby when she was upset. Sometimes when she was upset, I would squeeze her toes and she would laugh instead of cry. I would take each toe and squeeze it gently, and by the time I got to the tenth toe, she usually stopped crying.

It didn't work that time when the Mean Boy popped her balloon. I couldn't stop her crying that time. But usually the toe squeeze worked really well.

123

Dear Penny,

I don't want to talk to anyone, and I won't leave my room except to go to the bathroom. Wanna and Ellie try to get me to come out and do something with them, but I can't. Sitka came over but I told her to go away and that I didn't want to talk to her. I heard Wanna whispering something to Sitka when they stood by my door trying to get me to come out. I don't care.

Wanna brings me food to my room. Whenever she gives me something, she writes a note and tucks it into a napkin. She wrote at breakfast—

I know your heart is hurting right now. We are here for you.

And at lunch…

We love you, An-Ya. I am so sorry that you feel like you can't talk right now. We will wait until you are ready.

And at dinner...

An-Ya, I wish that I could make it all better. I am so sorry. I thought the journey to your sweet Abby, your Ye-Bi, would turn out differently. If only I could change so many things that were never in my control. You don't need to be alone with your feelings. Your family wants to help you.

124

Dear Penny,

Ellie keeps coming to my room to take care of Angel Bones. She knocks softly on the door and says—

An-Ya? I take Angel Bones to potty now, ok?

I never answer her, but she opens the door and Angel Bones runs to Ellie, and they walk out the door. When Ellie brings Angel Bones back, she doesn't say anything. She just opens the door and lets Angel Bones run in. Angel Bones is being very quiet. Somehow she knows that I need quiet.

I feel cold but I don't want to try to get warm.

I think cold is how I am supposed to feel.

Was I cold in the box that She left me in? Maybe that is why I don't want to get warm. I want to remember.

125

Dear Penny,

Last night I was tired of my soft bed and decided to crawl under my bed and lay on the hard floor. I imagined that I was on the floor in America, and when I looked up in the darkness that I could see all of Canada. I imagined that somewhere in the darkness above me was Abby's house and I could see her and I could see what she was doing.

I saw her on her tricycle going in circles. She was riding and worrying because crawling all around her were ladybugs and she didn't want to run over any of them. She didn't want to bring bad luck to her family by killing one of the ladybugs.

But then there was a bright light. Daddy turned my light on. I knew it was Daddy because I heard his voice—

An-Ya? An-Ya? Where are you?

And I didn't answer.

I didn't want to explain what I was doing under the bed.

He turned my light off, but he kept calling to me—

An-Ya?

And then he started yelling my name—

AN-YA?

My body tightened, but I didn't move or speak. I listened.

Daddy yelled my name and then he yelled Wanna's name and I heard shoes pounding on the hallway floor and up and down the stairs.

Someone was running. Then I heard Angel Bones barking. She was upset about the yelling and running.

I heard—

Where is she? Where is she?

But I don't know who was talking because voices started to mix together.

I could see Wanna and Daddy's feet standing next to my bed.

They were screaming my name into the air.

Angel Bones was barking and jumping at their legs.

Then Angel Bones became so worried that she ran under the bed and curled up over my head.

126

Dear Penny,

Angel bones gave my hiding spot away. After she curled herself around my head, then they knew where I was. Daddy knelt down on my bedroom floor and lifted the bottom of my quilt and saw me. His voice was soft and he said—

There you are, An-Ya.

Then Wanna knelt down beside Daddy and lifted the quilt too. Her voice sounded like she was talking through a whistle and she said—

You are safe. You are here. You are safe.

Wanna's eyes were red. I could tell even though it was dark. I didn't say anything back. I kept staring up and wondering how long it would take me to get to Canada if I started walking there now.

127

Dear Penny,

Daddy and Wanna stared at me lying under the bed for a long time. Ellie came in to stare at me too. Angel Bones stayed wrapped around my head but kept making little crying sounds.

Ellie said—

Are you sad, An-Ya, or are you on adventure?

I looked at her and then looked back up at the bed.

Ellie said—

If you on adventure, An-Ya, can I come? It is ok if we go on a sad adventure.

Then without me asking her to, Ellie crawled under my bed and lay next to me.

Then Wanna said—

I agree with Ellie. If you are on a sad adventure, then I would still like to join you.

Wanna crawled under the bed and put her arm across Ellie and settled her hand on my chest. Daddy followed them and crawled in on the other side and put his arm across my chest and joined hands with Wanna.

Wanna said—

An-Ya, please tell us what adventure we are joining you on tonight?

Finally words came out of me—

We are on a sad adventure. We are going back in time…to my orphanage in China.

They all moved closer to me as if we were really going back. As if they might lose me again. The tighter they held me, the more scared I became. I could smell them—Daddy, Wanna, Ellie, and Angel Bones. They all smelled so different, but together their smell mixed into something like apple juice and green grass. They were warm and I could feel their hearts beating against me.

I freed one arm from under their embrace, and I lifted it to the metal frame of my bed.

I began tapping.

I told them—

If you want to come with me, then you need to tap too.

One by one they all reached up their hands and began to tap.

I closed my eyes and listened. For a long time we tapped and listened to our fingers making music on the metal frame. We tapped until the metal frame of my bed became the metal frame of Abby's crib in the orphanage.

Then I stopped tapping. Then they stopped too.

I kept my eyes closed but I opened my mouth to talk. I told them we were back in the orphanage. I told them that our sad adventure back in time had begun.

128

Dear Penny,

It is morning now. I am in my bed under the covers. Ellie and Angel Bones are in my bed too and they are still quietly snoring. I don't remember everything that I said last night.

What I do remember is that I talked about taking care of Abby in the orphanage. How I was the one responsible for taking care of her and how much that bothered me sometimes. But there were also times that Abby gave me a reason to keep breathing. She needed me. And now she doesn't...or maybe she does...but now I will never know. Just because she has new ladybug clothes and a bicycle doesn't mean that she is really being taking care of, right? The photo doesn't tell me anything about how she is feeling inside.

While I was talking last night, Ellie and Angel Bones fell asleep curled around me. They both snored, but it was a quiet and soft kind of snore. But Daddy and Wanna listened all the way until I was finished talking.

I told Daddy and Wanna a little bit about my dreams and night-mares about the orphanage. I talked the most about the ones that included Abby.

I wanted to stop talking and suck back in all of the words that had already come out. But I couldn't do it. I kept going on and on like my mouth had a broken zipper.

Every once in awhile, as I was talking, Daddy would squeeze my hand or Wanna would run her fingers through my hair. I kept my eyes closed the entire time.

When I finally stopped talking, Wanna and Daddy were silent and waited to make sure that I was finished.

Then Daddy whispered—

Ok Baby Girl, let's get you out from under here and into your bed. It has been a long night for you and it is time for rest.

His arms reached under my body and pulled me out from under the bed and placed me on top of the bed and slid me under my covers. I felt heavy in my body and tired by my memories.

Wanna pulled Ellie and Angel Bones out and placed them on top of the bed next to me. They didn't wake up.

Daddy and Wanna looked at each other as if they were unsure of what they were supposed to say next. I didn't care what they said. I just wanted to close my eyes again.

Wanna said—

Good night, An-Ya. Thank you for taking me on an adventure with you, even if it was a sad adventure. Knowing your past helps me understand.

I thought she was going to start crying because her breathing became heavy and her voice was breaking.

Daddy said—

Good night, Baby Girl. Wishing you sweet dreams.

He blew me a kiss that I didn't return.

And then they were gone and I was left with the two small snoring bodies that slept through most of my sad adventure and didn't seem like they were about to wake up anytime soon. I was too tired to figure out how to move them.

How strange that Daddy called me...Baby Girl?

It doesn't feel like I have ever been a baby girl. To anyone. Ever. It feels like as soon as I was put in that box by Them that I became a person just trying to live and figure out how to keep living to the next day. Baby Girl? I was never a baby as far as I can remember.

But for a moment, as Daddy was holding me, I believed that maybe I could be a baby girl. Maybe the baby in me is not gone forever. Maybe it has been inside me all along.

I am tired. I need to go back to sleep.

129

Dear Penny,

Wanna made us chocolate chip pancakes this morning and she smiled at me a lot. The pancakes tasted very good, and smelled wonderful, but Wanna smiling so much was uncomfortable. Ellie kept saying how yummy to her tummy the pancakes were. It was a little cute the first time she said it, but she kept going on and on during the entire meal.

After pancakes I asked Wanna to borrow some of her poetry books. She didn't ask me why. She just smiled again, pulled some books off of the hallway shelves, and handed them to me. I tried to smile back at her, but I know my smile was much smaller than hers.

I took the books to my room and studied the ones that I could understand. Many of the poems were written in this old style of English and I couldn't tell what the poem was even about.

I didn't read all of them because most of them were boring. None of them seemed to be written about how I felt about Levi.

There was this one poem that I liked that was written by an American poet. It was interesting that the poet didn't use capital letters even when he signed his name. The poem was about carrying someone else's heart inside of them. But it wasn't exactly right for my situation. I think it was more meant for someone grown up and in love for a long time. Plus it said 'my darling' in the poem and that would just be weird to say to Levi. I don't want him to think that I am crazy. I just want him to understand that he is important.

130

Dear Penny,

I think I finally figured out what I have to tell Levi and how I want to tell him. For some reason reading all of the American poetry that Wanna gave me reminded me of a poem I once read in China. I hope that sharing this poem from China with him is the right thing to do because I have no idea what I am doing.

131

Dear Penny,

Sitka came over today. She was dressed in all red and it seemed like she was dressed to be going somewhere important. So I asked her if she was going somewhere special today. She looked confused and asked me why I would think that. I told her that she was wearing all red and that red was a happy celebration party color in China.

She said—

An-Ya, this isn't China, and I am just wearing red because I like it.

I just said—

Ok.

In America red is just red and nothing more. I should know that by now.

Sitka's parents were working at the hospital and she wanted us to take Angel Bones for a walk. That was ok with me because I didn't want to think about Abby and all the things that I told Wanna and Daddy when we were under my bed.

We walked through the woods and toward the covered bridge. I was thinking about what I was going to write to Levi and didn't realize I was walking ahead of Sitka. She yelled out to me—

AN-YA! Hold your horses and wait for me to catch up!

I asked her what she meant about the horses and she said it was called an idiom. Then we walked together and Sitka went on to teach me more idioms, like kick the bucket and spill the beans and…

I am on cloud nine…which I am not. But I think I made it to cloud seven or eight when Levi held my hand.

132

Dear Penny,

Ellie's birthday is tomorrow and Wanna is taking me shopping to get a birthday gift. I don't know what I should get her. Wanna suggested a doll, or a game, or some kind of toy she could play with. I don't want to get her any of those things.

What I really want to do is write my letter to Levi, but right now I am still thinking about what exactly I want to write. I just know that I want to be able to hand it to him the next time I see him and get it over with. He will either like it or hate it or still like me or maybe hate me.

Sitka better be right about this poetry and letter writing idea.

133

Dear Penny,

I bought Ellie her birthday present. We went shopping in a huge store that had two floors and an escalator. I tried to hide how nervous I was stepping on and off those moving stairs. The only other time I was on an escalator was in the airports coming home from China. I was pushed onto the airport escalators by the crowds behind me. I don't know if I would have ever left China if those strangers behind me didn't force me to step on.

Wanna and I went first to the toy section and looked at all of the toys. Wanna kept trying to get me to buy things that weren't what I wanted to give. In the toy area there was a little girl who was holding a fancy doll and screaming at her mom that if she couldn't buy the doll, then she wouldn't ever be good again. I wanted to take the doll and hit the girl over the head with it.

I finally found what I wanted to buy Ellie in the jewelry section. Wanna told me that it is called a charm bracelet. The bracelet has a silver chain and each of the chain loops has a little charm. All of the charms are tiny animals. There is a monkey, panda, flamingo, penguin, and hippo. The only charm that isn't an animal is a blue flower that sparkles.

Wanna said the bracelet was perfect. I hope Ellie likes it. I don't know why, but I really want her to like it.

134

Dear Penny,

Today was Ellie's birthday party.

Wanna gave me some wrapping paper decorated with bright colored flowers. It matched the tiny blue flower charm that was on the bracelet.

It was raining and the air was cool. I tucked the present box into my sweater pocket. I didn't want to put it on the pile of gifts waiting for Ellie to open. I wanted to hand the gift to her myself.

Ellie had a fairy party and invited a few of her little friends. Wanna gave all of the children fairy wings and a wand. I did not wear the wings or carry a wand, but I did let Ellie put some silver fairy dust on my face.

Even though it was raining outside, it felt bright and colorful inside the house.

Daddy couldn't come to the party because he had a work meeting to go to. He said it was very important and could mean good things for our family if it went well.

Wanna stood in the kitchen and offered food to all of the mothers who brought their children to the party.

The children were crazy and ran around our house swinging their wands and pretending to grant wishes or trying to turn our furniture into pumpkins. One little girl tried to turn me into a pony because she said it was her heart felt wish to have a pony. I tried not to laugh at her because she really seemed to think that it might be possible if she waved that wand hard enough.

Ellie looked happy. Her face was sparkling with fairy dust and her silver wings matched her silver and pink fairy dress. Everyone gathered together in the living room to watch Ellie open her presents. She opened her gifts so fast that I only knew what she received because after ripping off the wrapping paper, she would hold the present over her head and say—

This is a great present. Thank you very much!

Wanna told her before the party that she needed to thank the giver of each present before she opened the next one. Ellie did a good job and didn't forget to thank a single person for their present.

When all of the presents were opened, except mine, she turned to Wanna, clapped her hands, and said—

Now, Mommy will tell my birthday story!

Wanna looked confused and said—

What story is that, Ellie?

And Ellie said—

You know, Mommy. Tell everyone about the day that I came out of your tummy and I was born!

Everyone stared at the floor or at their feet. The room became totally quiet.

I will tell you the rest tomorrow. I guess you already know that it didn't go very well after that.

135

Dear Penny,

Ellie asked to hear about the day that she was born, and Wanna looked like she didn't know what to do.

Finally, Wanna ended the silence and quietly said—

Ellie, don't you remember how we talked about that you were born in China? Don't you remember the books that we have read about children who were born in China and then they were adopted?

Ellie looked angry. I have never seen that look on her face before. She said to Wanna—

Those were books, Mommy. I am not a book.

Wanna said—

I know you are not a book, but the story the books told is like the story of your life.

Ellie became even angrier and she said with a loud voice—

I don't want you to talk about books, Mommy! I want you to tell my friends about my day I was born!

Wanna looked like she was lost and she didn't know which way to go. She looked around the silent room and tried to apologize to everyone with her eyes. She said—

Ellie. You were born in China and I wasn't there, honey. You were born from your China Mama's tummy...not mine. I don't know the story to tell your friends. Only your China Mama knows the story of the day you were born. We have talked about this before. I think we should have cake now. Are you ready for some cake?

Ellie was not ready for cake. She fell to the floor and curled up in a ball and started screaming.

136

Dear Penny,

Nobody moved when Ellie started to scream. I was still in my chair and watching it all happen. Ellie was on the floor and there was a room full of people pretending that they weren't there at all.

Before I knew what I was doing, all of the sudden I was on the floor next to Ellie. I don't remember caring what anyone in the room thought about me or about the situation.

I touched Ellie's little back and began to rub my hand up and down. There was only a small part of her back that I could reach since she was wearing those fairy wings.

I whispered into Ellie's ear—

I was born in China too. I also have a mother in China that gave birth to me. I don't know my birthday story either. I don't know anything about the day I was born.

Ellie stopped screaming and looked at me. She said—

Truth An-Ya?

I stopped whispering and said to Ellie—

Yes, Ellie. That is the truth. We both do not know our birthday story, and we both have a mother in China that we don't know.

Ellie sat up. She looked so small and sad sitting there wearing her crooked fairy wings. Some of her black hair looked glued by tears to her cheeks. She asked me—

Why, An-Ya?

I told her that I didn't know why. I told her that I wished I knew why, but I didn't know the why about any of it for either of us.

Then I told her that I had a present for her that was still in my sweater pocket. I asked her if she wanted to open it. She nodded her head yes. I pulled the flower wrapped box out of my pocket and handed it to her.

She opened it slowly. People started to lift their eyes from the floor and stare at us as if they were waiting to see what would happen next.

Ellie pulled the charm bracelet out of the box, studied it for a minute, and then held it over her head to show everyone. She said—

Thank you An-Ya for this beautiful present. Thank you very much!

She hugged her bracelet and then asked me to help her put it on her wrist. Then she turned to Wanna and asked—

Mommy, birthday song now?

Wanna looked tired and she kept wiping her eyes with her shirt sleeve, but she smiled at Ellie and said—

Yes, Ellie. Now we will sing the birthday song.

Wanna started to sing, and then everyone in the room began to join in.

Ellie's fairy dust was sparkling around her chin, having been washed lower down her face by her tears. But once the singing began around her, she lifted her head high and smiled big at everyone in the room.

Happy birthday to you, dear Ellie…happy birthday to you!

We did eat the cake after that. The cake was very good. It was chocolate.

137

Dear Penny,

Sitka came over today. She didn't come to the birthday party yesterday because she got in trouble and was being punished by her parents.

It was still cool and raining, so Sitka came to my room and we sat on my bed to talk. Ellie was busy playing with her birthday presents and didn't follow us the way that she normally would have.

Sitka said the other day she was reading the newspaper and found out that a special star was coming to the sky. The star was going to show up and it would only be able to be seen on one night. If you didn't see it on that one night, then it wouldn't be able to be seen for another five hundred years.

So Sitka said—

An-Ya, I totally had to see that star. I just couldn't live my life without seeing that star. It was that important to me.

I asked her why seeing a star was so important.

She said—

I can't explain it to you. I knew it was something I had to do and somehow it was going to mean something to my future. You just have to believe me that I needed to see it.

Well, I didn't understand at all what she was talking about, but I did understand why she got in trouble.

The star was going to be viewable in the middle of the night. So in the middle of the night, Sitka decided to climb out of her upstairs bedroom window. She took her binoculars and laid her body flat on her roof.

Her parents heard her open her window and climb out.

When they found her, they were not happy.

Sitka told me she was sure that she saw her star before her parents caught her out on the roof. She said the star was bright and blinking like no other star in the sky. Sitka said it was one of those things that you know you have to do and you take the punishment.

I told her I thought she was crazy, but inside I understood part of what she was saying.

Sitka said—

We all have a little crazy in us. So tell me—how was Ellie's party?

138

Dear Penny,

I told Sitka what happened at Ellie's birthday party. She said that she was disappointed that she missed all of the excitement. I told her it wasn't exciting to watch Ellie scream on the floor. She said—

I know, An-Ya. I just mean that what you did for Ellie was awesome!

I told her there wasn't anything awesome about what I did at all. I did what I needed to do to make Ellie calm down because nobody else was doing anything. Sitka said that she never thought about how hard a birthday might be if you didn't know anything about the day you were born or who gave birth to you.

She asked me if I wanted to find my parents in China. I told her that they probably didn't want to know me because they never came back to find me.

Then Sitka put her hand on my arm. I looked at her face and she looked like she felt sorry for me. She asked me—

If you did meet them, what would you say to them?

I stared back at Sitka and said—

I don't have anything to say to them. Plus, we don't even speak the same language anymore.

Sitka said—

Seriously, An-Ya? Nothing?

I said—

I can't think of anything right now, so yes, nothing.

139

Dear Penny,

It is late and I am in my bed with Angel Bones. She is sleeping with her ears tucked under both of her paws. It is like she is trying to make her dog world quiet.

I wish I could make my voice inside my head quiet.

After Sitka left today, Wanna came into my room and told me she wanted to talk about what happened at the birthday party.

She didn't say very much and she still looked tired. She kept touching her yellow hair and pausing as she talked.

She said—

There is a lot that I want to tell you, An-Ya...but most of all I want to thank you for helping your little sister on her birthday. Ellie needed you... and you were there for her in a way that nobody else in that room could have been. It was...a brave thing that you did. I should have done more... and I should have thanked you sooner. I should have at least come to you both when you were on the floor...I don't know why I didn't...I want to apologize.

Wanna stopped talking.

She put her hands on my face and wrapped her fingers around my cheeks. Her hands were soft and they made my whole body feel warm. She asked me to forgive her if I could.

I said—

You don't know why you didn't do anything...and I don't know why I did do something.

Wanna nodded and removed her hands from my cheeks and rubbed my shoulders. Then she said good night and wished me sweet dreams and was gone.

Now I am awake thinking about why I helped Ellie when all of those people were watching. Why did I feel warm inside when Wanna held my face in her hands? And I wonder about Sitka's question about what I would say to my parents in China if I met them someday. I must have something that I want to say to them?

I can't stop thinking, but all I want to do is to stop thinking. Maybe I should cover my ears like Angel Bones and hope it will make my world quiet.

140

Dear Penny,

I think my brain was so busy last night that it stopped working all together and I fell asleep.

I wish I could talk about all of these problems with Levi. There is something about him that makes me feel like he will understand. Not that he could understand it all, but I think he could understand some of it.

Sitka is great to talk to, but she never seems to have any problems other than getting caught sitting on her roof in the middle of the night.

I don't know, Penny. Maybe I am making things up about Levi that don't really exist. Maybe I will look like a stupid girl trying to write him a letter about poetry.

But today I am going to write it anyway. I need to know if he is as real as I am hoping. I need to know one way or another and then move on.

141

Dear Penny,

I worked all day on writing to Levi. I wrote a lot and then threw it all out and then started over and over again. Finally, I am finished. Now all I need to do is hand it to him and wait to see if he runs away or not.

Here is what I wrote:

Levi,

I want to share some things with you. I have thought a lot about what I want to say and about what I want you to hear.

In China I lived in an orphanage. You probably know that about me even though we never talked about it.

Well, when I was in the orphanage, I remember finding this old book. I found it in a closet that was used to keep some of the cleaning supplies. I was reaching for a bucket on the floor and I saw this old book.

This might seem strange to you because in America everybody has books. But in China I didn't see very many books other than my school books. So finding a book on the floor of the cleaning closet was a big surprise.

Like I said, it looked old, plus it smelled old and the pages were stained. But it was special to me to discover it. I tucked the book under my shirt and took it somewhere quiet to read.

The book turned out to be a poetry book. Most of it was difficult for me to understand. But there was this one poem that I liked a lot and I felt like I understood it.

I can't read and write Chinese anymore, and even if I could I don't remember all the lines of the poem. I only remember the meaning.

So the meaning of the poem is what I would like to share with you—

The poem was about a man. He was a man who made many mistakes and bad decisions. All of the bad things that he did hurt people that he cared about. The people that he hurt were people who cared about him too.

The man didn't like who he was anymore. He decided to try and take the pain away from the ones that he hurt.

He made a tray full of food. He took the food to all of the houses where the people he hurt lived. He asked each person to please place the pain he caused on his tray of food.

All of the people he hurt did what the man asked. They pulled the pain from their hearts and placed it on the man's tray of food.

When the man was finished visiting all of the people that he hurt, he went back to his house. He took all of the food on the tray, with all of the pain added to the food, and he ate it. He ate everything on the tray. No crumb was left.

From that day on, the man was always sick to his stomach. The pain stayed inside of his belly and swam around. If he ate more food, he felt sick. If he didn't eat, then he felt sick too. The man accepted his punishment for all of his bad decisions that hurt all of the people he cared about.

The man became very sick and stopped leaving the house.

Then one day, two of the people that he hurt knocked on the man's door. They said they hadn't seen the man in a long time and thought maybe he might need something good to eat. The man looked awful and felt awful, but he took the food offered to him and said thank you and closed the door.

Then something strange happened. His door was knocked on again and again, and there was more food offered to the man by the people that he had hurt.

The man accepted all the food offered to him, and although he was scared of the food and how it might make him feel, he began to eat.

After eating the new food, made by the people who kept caring about him, his stomach began to feel better.

What he didn't know was that the pain he swallowed inside was now being pushed out of his stomach by the new food and the pain began entering his veins. The pain started traveling through his veins straight from his stomach to his heart.

Soon the man could then eat without pain. But his heart ached now. All of the pain was removed from his stomach and stuck in his heart. The pain in his heart was awful at first. But after some time passed, his body grew healthy again, and his heart learned to live with the pain. And even though the pain stayed in his heart, other feelings came inside his heart too. Some of those feelings were good feelings and softened the pain of his heart.

The end.

Levi, I think you might be one of the people in my life now who are helping me to move my pain from my belly to my heart.

I don't know if any of what I wrote will make sense to you. I will give you two choices—

1. You think I am crazy and walk away now. Please rip up this letter into one thousand pieces. 2. You don't think I am crazy, but rip this letter up into one thousand pieces and keep the story inside of you the way the story is inside of me.

—An-Ya

142

Dear Penny,

Do you think my letter to Levi is too long? I remember the poem in the old Chinese book was only a few pages. For some reason trying to explain and write about the poem took up more pages than the poem itself. Maybe because English writing takes up more space than Chinese?

I feel bad about what I wrote about Sitka not having any problems. It isn't really her fault, is it? She is one of those lucky people who have a life that has been good. At least she hasn't told me anything bad that has happened to her. Maybe I should ask her if there was a time when her life wasn't as good as it seems. She is always the one who asks all of the questions. Do you think I should ask her more questions back?

I am not sure how to be a friend to Sitka, so how could I possibly know how to be a girlfriend to Levi?

I have read my letter to Levi over and over and I can't think of a better way to explain what I want to say and what the poem means.

Now I need to wait until I see him again.

When Ellie hopes things will turn out how she wants, she says—

Mommy make waffles? Fingers crossed!

Mommy let Ellie wear fancy blue dress today? Fingers crossed!

Daddy give me piggy back ride? Fingers crossed!

So I say to you, Penny—

Levi understands my letter and doesn't laugh at me. Fingers crossed!

143

Dear Penny,

It is strange how my life right now is filled with letters. First, Wanna gave me the letter from Abby's parents. Second, I spent an entire day writing a letter to Levi. Third, Wanna came to me this morning to give me another letter. I didn't know what to think and was worried about what changes this letter would bring to my life.

Wanna still looks tired. It is something about her face color that makes me think she isn't sleeping well. Usually her cheeks are pink and shining, but now the pink is gone and her skin color is flat and pale.

She knocked on my door this morning and asked me if I had a minute to talk. I don't know why she thought I wouldn't have a minute. I told her it was fine to come in.

I was still in bed and wearing Wanna's robe. I was cold when I woke up and threw her fuzzy white robe around my shoulders.

Wanna was wearing a robe too. It was blue and matched her eyes. She sat on my bed and smiled at me. It was the kind of smile that was a question.

She was holding some papers, and it reminded me of when she shared the letters and news about Abby. Except this time Wanna didn't have so much worry on her face.

Wanna looked down at the papers in her hands and then she looked up at me.

She said—

An-Ya, you know that I was trying to figure out what happened to your Abby, your Ye-Bi, and I wrote letters to find out answers for you?

I said—

Yes?

She said—

Well, one of the places I wrote to was your orphanage. I have in my hands a letter from one of your nannies who cared for you. It seems that you were an important child in her life. I received the letter about a week ago, but of course, it was written in Chinese. It took a little time to get it translated. This morning I received the English translation.

Wanna looked down at the papers that she was holding. She kept looking at the papers and then looking at me. She smiled at me and then shook her head and then smiled at me again. Then she said—

I am going to give these to you and then go make some breakfast. We can talk about it all whenever you want to talk.

I said—

Ok.

Finally Wanna handed me the two pieces of paper. One of the papers was written in Chinese and the other was typed in English.

I didn't start reading right away. I first stared into Wanna's eyes, hoping to understand through her eyes if I should be afraid or not.

Wanna nodded her head at me and kept smiling at the papers. Her eyes told me to not be afraid. I didn't know what to expect. Who was writing to me from China? Why were they writing me? How would my life be different after I read this letter? My life felt so different after I read the letter from Abby's parents. I felt different inside after I wrote to Levi.

Wanna left my room.

I was scared but there was nothing else to do but read what was in front of me.

I will tell you about my letter from China after I eat. Right now I need to go eat something. My stomach is making strange noises and feels empty. I can smell that Wanna is cooking something sweet in the kitchen.

144

Dear Penny,

I was right that Wanna was cooking something sweet. She made crepes. It was my first time eating them. Wanna rolled up the thin pancake with strawberries and cream stuffed inside. On the top she sprinkled white sugar. Wanna said they were French.

Ellie ate breakfast with me. She didn't say anything because her mouth was full of crepes and strawberries. Ellie needs to learn how to use her napkin. It was hard for me not to take my own napkin and start wiping the food off Ellie's face.

Let me tell you about the letter from China. I have it in front of me and will copy it into your pages.

145

Dear Penny,

Here is the letter I received from China...

Hello, An-Ya,

It feels a long time since I have seen you. How are you? How is your health? I was happy to see that your America mother wrote to us. Now I can write to you and see how your life for you going. Is it good?

Do you remember singing with me as I played the old piano? Those memories are special for me to hold. Your song voice made all children stop their play and listen. You were our little singing bird. I miss you here with me singing.

Do you sing American or Chinese songs for your new family? They are lucky to listen to your voice now and must like to share your voice with American friends.

Things here are same. Ye-Bi was having difficult time without you. An-Ya, you remember boy with no eyes or hearing? Ye-Bi took care of him for a little time when you went to America. Ye-Bi help make him more calm. Ye-Bi was good little girl. You were a good big sister to Ye-Bi. She missed you very much. She is with new family now and maybe she is better and not always sad.

I miss you too. I am much relieved to receive a letter from your new mom asking about Ye-Bi and telling us that you are learning English fast. It is important. Try to keep your Chinese too so we can speak when you return to visit.

An-Ya, do you remember the day that you asked me to adopt you? I know I made a joke about it, but it was terrible for me. I cared about you deep inside. That night I went home and lost many tears about it. You are a special and smart girl. I knew it wasn't possible for you to be my daughter but I wished it to be different. Maybe I should not tell that story but I wish for you to know it.

Do you still have your pretty red journal? Maybe you will write in it some-day about your life here and you will write about me. I hope you will not forget me.

I know the story about you as a baby when you arrived here with your red journal. Whenever someone tried to take the journal out of your crib, you cried louder than all of the other babies. You would scream and not eat until they gave your red book back to you. Everyone learned fast that it was best way to let you keep your little journal. An-Ya, you were always a strong child. Please stay strong and be good in America.

Do not worry about your things kept in baby closets. I keep them there as reminder of you. An-Ya, you were a clever girl. I will not forget you. Your face is painted in my heart.

Wish all is well with you and whole family,

Ping-Hao

146

Dear Penny,

Were you surprised by Ping-Hao's letter? She still cares about me. She cares about you too. She called you my 'pretty red journal'. The story she told…about us when I was a baby…do you remember me crying for you? I never thought about how we stayed together for so long. We have always been together, and I didn't think about how or why that was. Even when I was a baby, I knew how important it was that we stay together.

I thought this would be another letter that would change me.

I was right.

I think I will read her letter one thousand times and still not understand exactly how I feel about what she wrote. I know that she says she will never forget me. She doesn't know that I have already written about her in your pages. She doesn't know that I will never forget her either. Her face is painted on my heart too.

What do you think Wanna thought when she read Ping-Hao's letter? She must have read it. I don't know. Wanna hasn't said anything about it since she gave the letter to me.

I am glad that Wanna gave me Ping-Hao's letter written in Chinese. I can't read it, but I like to look at Ping-Hao's handwriting and imagine her sitting at a table and writing to me.

147

Dear Penny,

It is after dinner and I am in the kitchen next to the fireplace. I like to sit here and watch the fire. The air outside is cool and the wind is blowing soft against the house windows. Every time I look at the fire, it changes. The fire is many colors…I can see white, yellow, orange, blue, and almost red.

My shoulders are warm and the house is quiet when the wind isn't blowing.

Daddy is here. Wanna is at a friend's house with Ellie. Wanna asked me to go with them, but I wanted to stay and write to you.

Daddy is working on his computer. He told me that he has some new projects that he needs to make perfect. He seems happy and excited about the new work. When Daddy talks about the new work with Wanna, she smiles or gives Daddy a hug and tells him congratulations.

Right now I can't hear the noise of his keyboard tapping under his fingers. The sounds made by the fire are louder than Daddy's tapping. I can feel him in the other room, but I can't hear him at all.

I have been thinking about everything that has happened recently. I am thinking the most about Ellie's birthday party and the letters.

What happened at Ellie's birthday party makes me wonder—

What if I knew nothing about my past before adoption? I mean, what if I didn't remember anything at all? What if I didn't remember anything about my life in China?

I have so many memories of my life in China. Ellie has none. Is it better to remember or to forget?

Wanna reads books about adoption to Ellie all the time. I have seen them cuddled together and reading stories about a little panda that was separated from its mother, but it found a wonderful new mother with a brown bear who loved it forever. There is this other story about a chicken, and it thinks it is a duck because the duck mother found the baby girl chicken and raised it like it was her own child. But one day it jumps into the water and tries to swim like the other duck sisters and it almost drowns. Don't you think the duck mother should have told the chicken that it wasn't a duck before it jumped in the water and tried to swim?

Wanna reads Ellie these stories, but it seems like Ellie doesn't understand that the stories are similar to her own story. It is like she doesn't know anything about her life before adoption and doesn't understand what adoption even means. Does Ellie understand that she is Chinese?

Maybe I don't remember the Chinese language, but I remember what it feels like to speak it off my tongue. Maybe that doesn't make sense, but I don't know how else to explain it.

I remember when everyone around me was Chinese, and I remember I never thought things would be different. In China I was Chinese and there would never be another way that I would need to learn to live. My only dream was for Them to come back and get me. When They did, I would have still been Chinese living in a Chinese world in China.

Now I am still Chinese, but I don't remember the Chinese language, and I am living in America. I am surrounded by people who don't understand anything about China except what they have read in a book or what small things my parents learned during their travels to adopt Ellie and me.

During my adoption in China, there were Chinese government people who were in charge of my adoption paperwork. They asked me—

An-Ya, do you want to be adopted and do you agree to this adoption?

Daddy and Wanna and Ellie were in the room, and I knew they couldn't understand what I was being asked. I remember looking around the room and wondering what would happen if I said—

No. I do not want to be adopted. Send me back to the orphanage.

But I didn't. I must have said yes. I didn't know then how the word *yes* could completely change everything that I knew about life. After that everything that I knew changed completely.

I was afraid. It was like I left my body, but my voice must have said yes. It is possible that my voice didn't say anything and my body nodded my head. I don't remember. Whatever I said or did must have meant yes. Because after my response, a government woman knelt down and took one of my feet and rubbed it in red ink. Then she lifted me onto a big table. My red painted foot was pressed onto my adoption papers. It was that red footprint stamp that began the end of my life in China.

Everyone in the room smiled and clapped.

I remember looking at my foot and thinking that the red ink on my foot would never go away. My foot looked like it was covered in blood. Wanna was given a wet towel and she scrubbed my foot and tried to wash it all away. She smiled up at me as she held my foot and tried to remove the red ink stain.

148

Dear Penny,

Wanna and Ellie are home and I am in bed and I am trying to fall asleep. I was thinking about something. I want to write it down before I forget.

Ellie was a baby when her little foot was painted in red ink. She didn't speak any language yet, so they must have never asked her if she was ok with her whole world becoming different. Her little foot was covered in ink and stamped red onto her adoption papers without her ever being asked if it was ok.

I feel like if I scraped the skin off of my foot deep enough that the red ink stain would still be there underneath. It is like the red ink stained my foot, but the red color is now covered over with new pink skin layers. I guess the red stain is underneath the skin of Ellie's foot too. She just doesn't know it is there yet. Maybe someday she will need me to tell her about it.

Abby's foot must be stained red underneath her skin layers too. I won't be there to let her know what it means.

All of us who were adopted must have the red stain underneath one of our feet. Even the Mean Boy must have it. The day that I was adopted, Wanna tried so hard to wash the red off, but I don't think the stain ever goes away completely. It is hidden, but it is still there underneath the layers.

149

Dear Penny,

This morning I was eating my oatmeal in the kitchen with Ellie. Wanna was wearing a new purple apron and cleaning the counters. All of a sudden, Wanna turned to me and said—

An-Ya, I didn't know you were a singer.

Wanna was looking at me like she was hoping that I would start singing right there and then. I knew these questions were coming my way someday, but I wasn't ready for them yet.

I said—

I used to sing sometimes.

Wanna said—

With Ping-Hao? Or did you sing other times too?

I said—

I didn't call her Ping-Hao. I called her my nanny.

She said—

Right. Maybe you called her the Chinese word for nanny, which I believe is...Ayi. It means something like an aunt in English.

I said—

That sounds right.

Wanna said—

So you only sung with your Ayi?

I said—

No, not always. Sometimes I was made to sing for other people.

Wanna was quiet for a minute, and I hoped she was done asking me questions. But she wasn't done. She said—

Were you happy singing for other people or just with Ping-Hao...your Ayi?

I said—

Ping-Hao. My Ayi.

Ellie said—

An-Ya is singer? That is so good, An-Ya!

Ellie was eating oatmeal, and the ends of her black hair were dripping into her breakfast.

I said to Ellie—

I am not a singer anymore. I sang Chinese songs and I don't remember them anymore. Can you please keep your hair out of your oatmeal bowl?

Ellie smiled at me and said—

I will help you, An-Ya. I teach you new songs!

I finished my oatmeal without looking at anyone. Then I took Angel Bones outside.

150

Dear Penny,

Nothing about today went the way that I dreamed that it would go. I took my letter for Levi outside with me and sat with Angel Bones under the willow tree. I waited.

I thought about showing Sitka the letter before I gave it to Levi. I even thought about showing it to Wanna. But after thinking about it a lot, I wanted Levi to be the only one to read it.

I played with Angel Bones. I threw her leaves and she chased them around as they blew in the wind. After a while I gave up hope that Levi would come. I was relieved because I decided the letter idea was not good. I was going to throw the letter out as soon as I went inside.

Then he was there. All of a sudden, Levi was on his bike in front of me. The letter was on the ground, and I was hoping he wouldn't notice. Why did I make the stupid decision to write LEVI in bright blue on the envelope?

Angel Bones was standing, with her tongue hanging out, right next to the letter in the grass. It was terrible. I couldn't speak or move.

Levi said—

Hey. You ok?

I tried to smile but only one side of my mouth would lift up.

And then he saw it. He looked at me and looked at the ground and looked at me again. Finally, he said—

So there is an envelope on the ground with my name on it. Am I supposed to pick it up or something?

I looked at Levi and watched him push his hair away from his eyes. He got off his bike and said—

Soooo I am going to pick up the envelope since it has my name on it. Ok?

I couldn't move or speak. I watched him pet Angel Bones and then he took the letter out of the grass and said—

Nowwww I am going to open the envelope that has my name on it. Ok?

After the envelope was opened, because I didn't jump and grab it out of his hands and run, he pulled the letter out and sat down to read.

I couldn't believe this was all happening. He was really here. He was really going to read the letter.

I sat down too because my legs were shaking, and I worried if I didn't sit down, I would fall down instead.

Angel Bones ran circles around us as Levi began reading my letter. I felt like I wasn't breathing well. It was like half of my lungs weren't able to fill up with air.

Levi stared at the first page. He turned all the pages over and then looked at the first page again. Then he looked at me and said—

This is a really long letter.

I looked at the ground and waited for him to get up and leave, but he didn't. He kept doing the same thing. He would look at the first page and then quickly turn the other pages over.

I couldn't understand what Levi was doing. I wished that he would either read the letter or get up and walk away. I tried to keep my eyes on the ground.

Levi whispered—

An-Ya? I can't read this.

I looked up into his eyes, not understanding what he meant.

There was hurt in his eyes and I wondered what I had done to give him pain.

I whispered back—

I don't understand?

He said—

It is my fault. I have this thing called dislexa. I can't make this letter make sense to me.

He shook the pages of my letter in front of me. I was lost and not understanding anything that was happening.

Again I whispered—

I don't understand?

He said—

It is my brain, An-Ya. It is hard for me to read and understand sentences and what they mean. My brain doesn't work right.

At first I worried that he was making a joke out of me. But his face told me that he wasn't joking at all. His face said that he really couldn't read what I wrote and understand it. His eyes were sad and frustrated.

Dislexa was a new word to me. It was a word that I now know causes Levi pain.

I need to go eat dinner now. I will finish writing to you later.

151

Dear Penny,

Since Levi couldn't read the letter, I thought that I should tear it up and start over with speaking.

Instead, Levi asked me to read the letter to him. He said that it would be faster that way. He said that for him to try to read it would take a long time.

I took a minute to think about it. I could read the letter or I could make up another letter and pretend like I was reading the real letter. It was a hard choice. The only problem was that I didn't know what to make up and pretend like I was reading at the same time.

I decided to read the real letter. I started reading it and Levi told me that I was too quiet and he couldn't hear me. So I spoke with a louder voice and read the whole thing without looking at him until I was finished.

When I was finished, Levi was sitting still and looking at me. Angel Bones was sitting next to Levi and staring at me too. I said—

What are you looking at?

Levi kept staring and said—

That was the weirdest letter I have ever heard in my whole life. Can you read it again?

He meant it. He wanted me to read it again. I didn't know what to think, but I started the letter all over again.

Levi asked me to read the letter four times. After the fourth time, he told me to hand the pages over to him. I did.

He looked at me and said—

I wish I could keep this.

I said—

You can't.

He looked at the pages one more time, and then he tore them into one thousand pieces. He threw them into the wind.

Angel Bones chased the paper flying all around us.

Levi wrapped his arms around me, and his hair pushed against my neck. When it was over, I could feel my shoulder was wet. He whispered into my neck—

I don't understand everything, but I do understand some things.

What did I do with my arms? I don't remember. Was he crying? It all happened so fast. And then he was back on his bike and gone.

I sat under the willow tree and tried to remember everything that happened with Levi. I didn't want to forget any of it.

152

Dear Penny,

After dinner, I asked Wanna how to spell *dyslexia* and if she knew anything about it. She said she only knew a little bit but asked me to come and sit with her at the computer and we could learn about it together. Wanna never asked me why I wanted to know.

I shared a chair with Wanna. We sat pressed against each other as she typed questions into the computer. Wanna was cleaning the wood in the house earlier, and she smelled like lemons.

I learned a lot about dyslexia. I learned that Levi was not alone. There are many people who are dealing with letters that don't look right and sentences that don't seem to be in the right order.

I asked Wanna if there was a name for why Abby looked the way that she did. What was the name for someone with white hair, white skin, and grey eyes that don't work very well?

Wanna told me that Abby had albinism. We looked on the computer at pictures of children and adults who had the albinism.

It was hard to look at all of those faces of people who had the same thing as Abby. It made me remember how afraid I was, in China, when Abby would get sick or if I couldn't find her in the orphanage. I didn't know if what she had, the thing that made her hair white and her eyes grey, was going to make her die.

Now I know that her body will be ok and the albinism won't kill her. But I still feel scared because I will never see her again to know for sure that she is ok on the inside.

She isn't my Abby anymore. She isn't my Ye-Bi in China. She is now a stranger to me. I am probably a stranger to her too.

I thought about telling Wanna what I have told you. The parts about being scared. But instead I said—

Thanks.

Wanna leaned her head down and placed it against mine. She said—

You are very welcome.

153

Dear Penny,

Wanna lets me borrow her music player to listen to before I go to sleep.

Wanna's player shows me the song it is playing. It tells me who wrote the song and the name of the song.

I have one song that I like to play the most.

When I listen to the song, I can see my dancers in my head. They dance with everything that they hold inside of them.

The dancers move slowly, but their feelings are fast. They wear long dresses that float around them when they turn.

The name of the song is 'Fly Away' and the singer's voice is soft and low when he sings—

For you are a rich gift from angels up high,

A wonder filled child, with bright sunny eyes,

A gem of the earth as you fly through the sky.

For you are a sweet child with bright sunny eyes,

A gem of the earth as you soar through the sky.

Fly away, fly away, fly away.

It reminds me of how I felt when I looked at the butterfly on the wall of the orphanage. I wanted to fly too. I still do.

154

Dear Penny,

Today I went to the market with Wanna and Ellie. Wanna needed some ingredients for a soup that she is making tonight.

I put Angel Bones on a leash and took her with us. Because I took Angel Bones with us, I wasn't able to go inside the market. No dogs are allowed inside. Wanna took Ellie in and I waited with Angel Bones outside.

Wanna told me before we left that I should wear a jacket, but I thought I would be fine. I wasn't. It was cool and my arms weren't covered. I picked up Angel Bones to keep me warm.

I tried not to look into the ice cream parlor window, but I couldn't stop myself. Jazz was inside serving her customers hot chocolate. I could see the steam and the whipped cream on top. She looked beautiful and happy and was wearing blue feathers in her hair.

In the back of the parlor, Levi was sitting with his brother Lex and they were playing a card game. As I turned to leave and go back to the market and wait for Wanna and Ellie, Levi saw me. I acted like I didn't see him and carried Angel Bones to the market next door.

Levi followed me. He came out of the parlor and stood in front of me. I didn't know what to say. He looked nice in jeans and a black jacket.

He said—

Are you cold, An-Ya? Do you want my jacket?

He started to take off his jacket and I said—

No. No, I am good.

He said—

I am working on writing you a letter back. It is taking me longer, though. You know?

I said—

That's ok. You don't have to do that.

Then Wanna and Ellie came out of the market. Levi said hello to them and kept talking to me—

I want to do it. So I will see you later?

I nodded my head and turned to walk home.

Wanna handed me a bag to carry and the way that she looked at me asked—

Are you sure about him?

I didn't answer.

Ellie said—

Levi's eyes like a rabbit. I like him.

Ellie waved at Levi as she walked away. He waved back and smiled.

I put the bag over my shoulder and held Angel Bones tight against me. I thought about if Ellie was right about Levi's eyes.

I don't think the eyes of a rabbit could make me feel the way that Levi's blue eyes do.

155

Dear Penny,

Wanna told me tonight that if I wanted to, I could write a letter back to my nanny Ping-Hao. She said that she could have my letter translated in Chinese and mailed to China.

At first, I was excited. But now I feel unsure. Whatever I write will be read by Wanna. I don't want to hurt Wanna, but the things I want to say to Ping-Hao might feel hurtful.

I need to think about it.

156

Dear Penny,

Sitka came over this morning and it didn't go very well. She knocked on the door while I was eating breakfast. Angel Bones barked and Wanna let Sitka into the house.

Sitka looked mad but pretty. Her hair was as straight as mine and her dark skin was shiny. She was wearing jeans that were decorated with small yellow flowers.

She told me that she needed to speak to me privately, so we went to my room to talk.

After she sat down on my bed, she was silent. Finally I asked her what we needed to speak about. She said—

I saw Levi on my way here. He was riding his bike. I asked him where he was going, and he said he was going home to finish writing a letter back to you.

Sitka pointed at me like I did something very wrong. I said—

Why do we need to talk about that?

She said back—

Because you didn't tell me anything about this! You never told me you gave him the letter. You never told me what the letter was about. You never told me what he said. You never told me ANYTHING! I THOUGHT WE WERE FRIENDS!

Sitka yelled the last part.

I didn't know what to say, so I stared at the quilt on my bed and studied all the fabric squares.

Sitka said—

You need to say something, An-Ya.

I looked up at her smooth hair and her brown eyes that matched her skin and said—

How did you get your hair that smooth?

Sitka touched her hair and said—

I put some stuff in it to make it straight, but you aren't answering my questions.

I said—

I like your hair that way. It's pretty.

Sitka still did not look happy. She said—

Why do you like it this way? Because it looks more like your hair?

I shook my head no. All of the sudden, I felt like I wanted to know more about Sitka.

So I asked her—

What is the worst thing that ever happened to you?

Sitka looked down at my quilt and rubbed the sewn lines along the quilt squares. When she looked up at me, she said—

I guess it was pretty awful that I was born with a hole in my heart.

I said—

What do you mean?

Sitka explained that she was born early and with a heart problem and needed to have surgery to fix it when she was a baby.

I told her I was sorry about her heart and asked her if there was something else that was awful in her life.

She said—

Well, my parents are always working and I don't see them very much. Their patients seem more important to them than I do sometimes. Having parents who are doctors is rough. It isn't awful…I mean, they are helping people and stuff. But it can be lonely.

I said—

Oh. Is that why you are here a lot?

Sitka said—

Yeah. Plus, I usually like it here.

I asked her if there was anything else awful in her life. She said—

There was that time when someone yelled out their car window at me and called me the N word.

I didn't know what she was talking about, so I asked—

What N word?

Sitka's brown eyes got big, and she looked at me like I was trying to make fun of her. She looked hurt.

She said—

Are you serious, An-Ya? You don't know the N word?

I told her I didn't have any idea what she was talking about.

She said—

It is a nasty word said by nasty people to black people like me. It is a word said to make African Americans feel like they are dirt.

I still didn't understand. She was staring at me and I felt like her brown eyes were going to burn a hole in my head. I said—

So the N word is about your skin color being so dark?

Sitka didn't answer but she kept staring at me.

I said—

Are you ok with your skin being so dark?

Sitka got off my bed and headed to my bedroom door. She looked back at me before she left and said—

I am totally fine with my skin color, An-Ya. In fact, I love my dark skin. Maybe you are the one with a problem?

Just as she was about to leave, she turned and stared back at me and said—

The N word stands for Nigger.

Then she slammed my door and was gone.

157

Dear Penny,

After Sitka left, Wanna came to my room and opened the door. She asked me what happened and why was Sitka leaving our house with tears in her eyes.

At first I told Wanna that nothing happened. But she didn't leave and kept sitting on my bed waiting for me to talk.

After I realized Wanna wasn't leaving until I said something, I told her—

I didn't try to make Sitka upset. I don't even know what I said that was so bad.

Wanna looked into my eyes. She was wearing new eye makeup, and her eyes looked bright and a little green. She said—

How about you try and tell me what happened and then I will try to help you figure out what went wrong.

So I did tell her. Well, not everything. I left out the part about Sitka being mad at me for not telling her about my letter to Levi. But I told her almost everything else. I even told her about the N word.

Wanna put her arm out and said—

Come on over here with me and sit and we will talk about all of this.

I said—

I am sitting here.

Angel Bones jumped up onto my lap.

Wanna said—

Ok, then sit there, but I would still like you to tell me more about what happened.

We started talking and I explained everything again.

Wanna said that asking Sitka if she was ok with her skin being dark would be like someone asking me if I was ok with being Chinese. By asking the question, it makes it seems like maybe there is something wrong about it.

I don't know if I am telling you about it exactly like Wanna told me, but it made sense. I understand now how I might have hurt Sitka without trying.

I said to Wanna—

There are people in China that think that being whiter is better.

Wanna said—

There are people in America who think the same thing. The same people who called Sitka the N word.

I looked up at Wanna and said—

I used to be one of those people who thought that.

Wanna reached over and held onto my shoulders. She looked down at me and said—

There is good and bad in all of us. Plus, I think I heard you say...you used to be one of those people? That means that it is not who you are anymore.

I nodded my head yes.

158

Dear Penny,

I fell asleep last night in Wanna's robe. I woke up sweating. It is very early morning and still dark outside.

I was dreaming.

Do you remember the boy in the orphanage who gave me my first kiss? He was the one whose face was half covered in red. I had a dream about him.

He was here in this house with me. He was sitting with me next to the fireplace in the kitchen. It was strange because he was wearing the clothes that Levi was wearing at the market...a black jacket and blue jeans.

His face looked like it was on fire. His red stain was so red that it looked like blood covered one side of his face, but I wasn't afraid.

I asked him if he was ok.

He said—

They keep giving me these pills to make the red go away, but it is making me even redder.

I asked him who? Who is giving him the pills?

He said his parents were giving him the pills because they thought he would be happier if the red went away. But the pills weren't working, and they were making it worse.

I asked him what he was going to do, and he said—

I think I will stop taking the pills. Maybe I will pretend to swallow them, but I will spit them out later.

He told me that he wanted to be able to look in the mirror and see the same person that he was in China. He didn't want to change his skin. He asked me if I thought he should keep trying the pills.

I said—

No. Don't take the pills anymore.

He said—

Do you want me to kiss you again?

And then I woke up. I pulled off Wanna's robe and climbed on top of my covers to cool down. Then I started writing inside your pages.

Now I feel cold. I need to get under the covers again.

159

Dear Penny,

I never knew what it meant to have a best friend until I lost one. I should have told Sitka everything about what happened with Levi. I thought I wanted to keep it inside me, but now that I don't have anyone to share it with. I realize that I was wrong. I want a best friend to share it all with, but now my best friend hates me.

Sitka said she was born early with a hole in her heart but the doctors fixed it. Maybe I was born with a hole in my heart too? Maybe nobody ever checked and I have a hole in my heart that is growing bigger each day? That would explain why I can't ever talk about everything inside of my heart, because it keeps falling out of the hole before I can explain it.

160

Dear Penny,

Daddy said that tonight we were going *to party*. He said that we weren't going to a party but we were going to create a party in our house.

Only our family was invited.

He ordered pizza to be delivered. We ate our pizza in the kitchen.

I am starting to like pizza. I used to hate it. I always liked the way it smelled, but the cheese felt weird in my mouth. I couldn't eat the cheese without feeling sick.

Now I am getting used to it and eating pizza doesn't make me feel bad anymore.

Daddy bought soda for me and Ellie. He gave us little umbrellas and straws to put in our drinks.

For Wanna and Daddy, there were red and white wine bottles to choose from.

We all were given fancy glasses to pour our drinks into.

Ellie was very excited and said—

I like our party Daddy!

Wanna filled her fancy glass with white wine.

Daddy picked red wine.

I chose soda with a straw but without the little umbrella.

Ellie wanted the soda, the straw, and the umbrella.

Daddy said that he wanted to make a toast.

I thought he was going to make toast, which seemed strange.

Instead he held his fancy glass up in front of his face and said—

I love that all of my girls are here with me to celebrate.

He smiled at all of us. Daddy's black hair was pushed back from his face, and his striped blue shirt and dark gray pants made him look very important.

Wanna was wearing a long black dress with peach flowers. Her skin looked like it matched the flowers in her dress. She smiled at Daddy and held her glass of wine in front of her smiling face.

Ellie was wearing a purple dress and black shiny shoes. She was holding her umbrella drink and smiling at Daddy too.

I was the only one wearing jeans.

Daddy said—

I love all of you and am so happy to be surrounded by you tonight. I can't believe how lucky I am. We are here to have our family party and to celebrate that I have received incredible new work contracts. I truly hope this means that we won't have to worry about money again for a long time.

Daddy looked like he was becoming king. I wasn't sure about anything that was happening. I knew that Daddy was happy, so I tried to be happy for him. He asked us all to raise our glasses and I raised mine.

Daddy said—

To us! To our family!

After that we were all tapping our fancy glasses against everyone else's glasses. Daddy and Wanna were drinking their wine and tapping their glasses against each other over and over again.

Then Wanna started to play music.

161

Dear Penny,

The party continued in the living room. There was a warm fire. Wanna's music was all around us.

The music was soft and slow.

Daddy and Wanna were dancing together, and they were very close. I thought that they were going to start kissing.

If they started to kiss, then I was going to go to my room right way.

Ellie looked up at me and said—

We dance now, An-Ya?

I looked down at Ellie and saw that she wanted me to do the dancing with her. Her arms reached out to me.

She wrapped her arms around my waist, and I placed my hands on her shoulders.

Ellie pressed her head into my belly and she tried her best to dance. But her shoes were slipping around on the wood floor and she couldn't move around without sliding.

She said—

An-Ya, new shoes slippery!

I looked down at Ellie's face. She was worried. I told her that it was ok.

I put my hands on Ellie's head and ran my fingers through her black hair. It was hair that I was once so jealous of, but now my hair was almost as long as Ellie's.

I said—

Ellie, you are a good dancer.

Her black eyes looked into my black eyes, and she smiled and said—

I good, but my shoes are not as good as me.

162

Dear Penny,

I don't know what to write. It is too terrible to write anything. I am at the hospital and I don't know how to write what has happened.

Ellie fell down.

After the party, Ellie and I said goodnight to Daddy and Wanna.

I grabbed you off of the living room book shelf, where I left you before the party.

Ellie ran up the stairs ahead of me. She was excited to get her pajamas on because Wanna promised to read her a bedtime story.

But she didn't make it all the way up the stairs before she slipped and fell all the way down.

I saw it happen. I saw her falling. But there wasn't anything that I could do to stop it.

She fell all the way to the bottom and landed at my feet.

Her fancy slippery shoes slipped on the wood stairs, and she fell backwards.

Ellie's head banged into the wood stair corners as she rolled down.

I didn't do anything. I watched it all happen, but I didn't do anything. It was so fast and I stood completely still. I wanted to move, but I couldn't. I held onto you and watched her tumble toward me without doing anything.

Ellie landed in front of my feet and she didn't make any noise. She looked like a black haired doll with closed eyes. Blood started running out of her nose.

Ellie might die. We are at a hospital, and I can't stop thinking about how it should be me with blood running out of my nose instead of Ellie. Ellie would have moved. She would have saved me somehow.

163

Dear Penny,

I am still at the hospital. Sitka is here now. Her parents came to try to help Ellie. When Sitka saw me, she ran to me and hugged me for a long time. We didn't say anything to each other, but there wasn't anything to say that would make it better.

Wanna and Daddy keep coming in, then leaving the waiting room to talk with the doctors and nurses.

Everyone is silent when they are in this room. Nobody is telling me what is happening to Ellie.

164

The hospital waiting room has brown walls and blue chairs. There is a plastic green plant in the corner. Sitka is curled up on a chair and is watching a small TV that is hanging from the ceiling.

I am sitting on the floor in a corner and writing to you. I want to get out of here, but I don't want to leave here without Ellie.

165

Dear Penny,

I must have fallen asleep. How did I fall asleep? Daddy woke me up and I was still in the waiting room. The TV hanging from the ceiling was turned off, and Sitka was asleep in a blue chair.

Daddy told me that we were going home, and I said—

No.

Daddy whispered to me that Ellie was having an operation to help her brain get better. Ellie's brain was bruised and there was some bleeding inside that the doctors were trying to stop.

Daddy told me that we needed to go home and get some rest. There wasn't anything that we could do at the hospital to help. We needed to go feed Angel Bones and let her go to the bathroom. He said we would come back after we rested and the operation was finished. I said—

No. I can't leave.

Daddy put his arms around me and lifted me up and told me that we were leaving. Daddy said Wanna was staying at the hospital, but I didn't know where Wanna was.

It felt wrong to leave, but Daddy looked like someone very different than the I knew a few hours ago at the party. The look in his eyes filled me with fear.

I pointed to Sitka and said—

What about her? Why does Sitka get to stay?

Daddy told me to wake up Sitka, and he left the room for a few minutes.

Sitka was hard to wake up. I talked into her ear and kept telling her—

Sitka! Wake up!

When she finally woke up, she didn't seem confused. It was like she was used to sleeping in that blue chair.

Daddy came back to the waiting room and said that Sitka was coming with us.

166

We are home now, and Sitka and Angel Bones are sleeping in my bed. I can't sleep. I want to stay awake until Daddy tells me that we can go to the hospital and bring Ellie home.

167

I am still awake and waiting.

168

Dear Penny,

I am still awake. I don't know how to sleep when doctors are cutting Ellie's head open. Plus, Sitka keeps kicking her legs over mine.

I can feel that Ellie and Wanna aren't here. I don't know how to explain it other than to say the house feels emptier and colder. I have never slept in this house without Wanna and Ellie. Wanna's robe is wrapped tight around me, but I can't get warm enough.

169

Dear Penny,

Daddy came into my room when the morning sun started to come through the window. I said—

Can we go get Ellie now?

He told me that it might be many days before we could bring Ellie home. He rubbed his eyes and pushed his hair out of his face and tucked the longer pieces behind his ears. Daddy didn't look well. He looked pale and red patches covered the skin on his neck.

I let Sitka sleep and took Angel Bones outside to go to the bathroom and came back in and filled her food bowl. Even Angel Bones seemed to know that something was wrong. She always wags her tail when I give her food, but her tail didn't move at all this morning.

Sitka was awake when I came back to my room. She asked me if there was any news about Ellie, and I said—

I don't know. I was too afraid to ask.

We got dressed. Sitka borrowed some of my clothes. The only thing that fit her was a yellow dress with long sleeves that I never wore. Everything else was too small. Sitka looked good in the dress and I told her to keep it.

Sitka looked at herself in my bedroom mirror and agreed that she looked nice in my dress. She kept looking in the mirror but said to me—

Do you remember when we first met and I told you that I was named Sitka because my mom gave birth to me under a Sitka tree?

I nodded my head but I didn't understand why she was talking about that now.

She said—

It wasn't true. I just tell people that. I was born in a hospital. My mom just likes the name Sitka.

I didn't say anything because Daddy came into my room. He asked us to get something quick to eat and that we would go in a few minutes. Sitka was going to her house because her parents were home now and they were resting after helping with Ellie's surgery.

170

Dear Penny,

We dropped Sitka off. She hugged me again and whispered in my ear that she would be praying for Ellie all day. I am not sure how the praying thing works, but it can't hurt, I guess.

I whispered back to Sitka—

I didn't mean to hurt you.

Sitka didn't answer me, but hugged me tighter, then got out and closed the car door.

I am back in the waiting room and sitting on the floor in the corner again.

There is a man and a woman on the other side of the room. They are sitting in the blue chairs, and they are crying. I have no idea what happened to them.

I still can't believe that this is all real because it doesn't seem real at all.

Daddy left me here to go check and see when we would be able to see Ellie. I haven't seen Wanna yet.

Why do you think Sitka made up that story about being born under a tree?

171

Dear Penny,

I am still waiting for Daddy to come back. I tried watching the TV attached to the ceiling, but it was a show about cooking, and I kept thinking about Ellie and Wanna together laughing in our kitchen.

The night that Ellie fell down the stairs feels like a dream that I can't forget.

Wanna and Daddy must have heard Ellie fall because right after Ellie stopped moving, they were both there next to us.

I remember hearing screaming, but it wasn't me screaming. It must have been Wanna.

I remember someone saying—

Don't move her. Don't move her. No! Don't move her!

Is she breathing? Can you hear her heart beating?

Then there was more screaming, but it was a quieter scream.

Daddy turned to me and said—

Go call 911 right now. Now. Go.

I don't remember picking up the phone or dialing.

Wanna taught me so many safety rules when I first came here, and calling 911 was one of them. She also taught me stop, drop, and roll for a fire. There was a stranger danger lesson for not getting myself stolen. I learned about how not to swallow and get poisoned by cleaning liquids. Wanna told me not to put plastic bags over my head because I might not be able to breathe. Not that I wanted to cover my head in plastic bags, but she told me anyhow.

I never imagined that I would need to use anything that she taught me.

But I did somehow call 911 and a woman answered and asked me—

What was my emergency?

I told her my sister fell down the stairs.

The woman asked me a lot of questions like—

Is my sister talking? Is she breathing? Is she bleeding? Is she moving? Is her heart beating? Who is there with you?

It was so many questions that I can't remember them all. I do remember the 911 woman saying—

Tell your parents not to move her. Help is on the way. I am here for you. Sweetheart, stay on the phone with me until the ambulance arrives. Look out the window, and you will see the ambulance lights coming very soon.

Then the 911 woman said—

Sweetheart, are you still there?

I answered—

I see the lights.

Then I hung up.

172

Dear Penny,

Daddy came to get me in the waiting room. He said we could go in and see Ellie for a few minutes, but that she was sleeping and we wouldn't stay long. I want to see Ellie, but I am afraid about what she will look like.

173

Dear Penny,

Ellie is in a hospital room and attached to a lot of machines that beep.

She was sleeping on a bed that is much bigger than she is.

She was wearing a purple dress with pink elephants that the hospital gave her. She had a tube stuck in her mouth that Daddy said was filling her lungs with air. Her head looked like it was wrapped in white fabric. I couldn't see any of Ellie's black hair.

Wanna was sitting next to Ellie's bed and singing to her. She was still wearing the black dress with peach flowers that she wore to our family party. Either the dress looked like it got bigger, or Wanna shrunk inside of the dress. She was pale like Daddy. It took a minute for Wanna to notice that I was there in the room.

When she saw me, she stopped singing to Ellie and turned toward me. She said my name and wrapped her arms around my neck.

I put my arms around Wanna's waist. She kissed my head all over as if she was making sure that my head wasn't broken too.

The way that Wanna held me reminded me of the night that I found out about Wanna's car accident. It reminded me that underneath Wanna's black flower dress was her upside down T shaped scar.

I asked Wanna if I could talk to Ellie or did I need to wait for her to wake up?

Wanna said that I could talk to Ellie but to use a quiet voice.

I let go of Wanna and went to Ellie. There were so many machines and needles connected to her little arms. I didn't know if it would hurt her to touch her.

Ellie's cheeks looked bigger, and her eyes and lips were puffy.

I decided to lean over her small body and whisper into her ear.

I said—

Ellie, don't be scared. You will be better soon. When you come home, we will teach Angel Bones a new trick. Fingers crossed, ok?

I never noticed how long Ellie's eyelashes were before. Her swollen eyes were closed, but her eyelashes moved a tiny bit.

174

Dear Penny,

Daddy and I spent the day going back and forth to the hospital. We brought Wanna clean clothes and clean underwear for Ellie. Wanna gave us a list of things to bring to the hospital so that she could continue to stay with Ellie. There is an extra little bed in Ellie's room that Wanna can sleep in. Wanna also wanted her toothbrush and her makeup case.

Most of the time, there were doctors or nurses coming in and out of Ellie's room. I spent a lot of time in the waiting room.

Sometimes I was alone in the waiting room, and sometimes other people would come in and sit in the blue chairs.

Nobody ever laughed in the waiting room. People didn't do much talking at all. Some people looked down at the floor. Some pretended to watch the TV. Some people looked at one another. Many of the people looked like they were going to cry. Some of the people did cry.

I kept myself busy by making up stories in my head about the people in the waiting room.

Daddy walked in and out of the waiting room all day long. When it was dinner time, he told me it was time for us to go home for the night. He said that I could go into Ellie's room and say goodnight to Ellie and Wanna.

I told Daddy that I would rather just go home and see them tomorrow.

175

Dear Penny,

It is morning and I am still feeling tired.

Last night Daddy stopped on the way home from the hospital and bought us cheeseburgers and french fries.

I didn't think that I wanted to eat, but once I smelled the food in the bag, I realized that I was very hungry.

I ate all my food in the car before we even made it home.

After I took Angel Bones out to the bathroom and fed her, and said good night to Daddy, I put on Wanna's robe and lay in my bed. I thought that I would fall asleep right away. I felt tired on the inside and outside. But I couldn't fall asleep.

I was still hungry. I remembered my bottle in the kitchen and went downstairs to fill it with milk.

Walking on the stairs scared me. I felt like I was stepping on Ellie's body with every step that I took.

I went into the kitchen and searched for my bottle. It was a long time since I last used it. I couldn't find my bottle, but I found one of Ellie's. I warmed up the milk in the microwave and poured it into her bottle.

I was about to go back to my room when Daddy came into the kitchen. He was wearing red plaid pajamas that I never saw him wear before and holding a glass of wine. He asked me if I was ok.

I said—

Yes. I am getting some milk.

He looked at the bottle and looked at me.

He said—

Is that Ellie's?

I said—

Yes.

He said—

Come and sit with me in the living room and we can watch my favorite show together.

I didn't know if I should take Ellie's bottle with me or not. But Daddy said—

Don't forget Ellie's bottle.

So I picked up the bottle and we went into the living room and we sat on the sofa together. Daddy was watching a TV show about fixing up old houses.

I wasn't sure about drinking from the bottle in front of Daddy. My stomach was making strange noises, and I decided I would drink from the bottle and not worry about what Daddy thought about it.

As I began to drink my milk, Daddy asked me to sit closer to him so that we could talk about things.

He put his arm around me, and my head leaned against his heart.

His pajamas were fuzzy and his voice was soft like wind blowing through the willow leaves.

He said—

Are you ok An-Ya?

I said—

I don't know.

He said—

What are you afraid of?

I said—

That Ellie won't ever be able come home.

Then Daddy started to tell me that Ellie will definitely come home. He said that Ellie needed to have a small hole cut in her head because when she bumped her head on the stairs, the inside started bleeding. But he said the bleeding was stopped now, and the extra blood was taken out through the little hole they made.

He told me that because her head bumped into the stairs, it got a little swollen inside too. He said the doctors made a hole inside Ellie's head to help the doctors see inside and know when the swelling gets better.

Daddy said that is why Ellie is getting extra help breathing. When the swelling in her brain goes down, then she will start to breathe again on her own.

I drank my milk from Ellie's bottle and listened to Daddy talk, and then he was finished. He stopped talking and watched his show, and I tried to watch too. But I was too tired to watch. So I closed my eyes and listened.

I must have stopped listening to the show because the last thing that I remember hearing is Daddy's heart beating softly in my ear.

176

Dear Penny,

You won't believe what happened today. I was finishing getting dressed to go to the hospital when I heard someone knocking on the door. Angel Bones started barking. I threw on a blue sweater and went to the front door.

Guess who was standing there?

It was Jazz, Lex, and Levi.

When I opened the door, they all started to talk at once and told me how sad they were to hear about Ellie's accident. I wasn't sure how they heard about it, but somehow they did.

Jazz handed me big warm lasagna. She told me that her mother made it for us since she knew we must be busy with trips to the hospital.

Lex gave me flowers for Ellie, and Levi gave me flowers for me. Plus, Levi gave me a letter.

I stood there with all of their gifts piled in my arms and said—

Thank you.

Daddy yelled out from the living room—

Is everything ok An-Ya? Are you ready to go?

I yelled back—

Yes. I will be ready in a minute.

Jazz, Lex, and Levi all said to tell Ellie that they were praying for her and that they hoped she felt better soon.

I said I would tell her when I got to the hospital.

They each gave me a hug, and I stood very still since my arms were full and I would have died if I dropped their gifts. Levi's hug was the strongest.

After they left, I put the lasagna in the fridge. I thought we could heat it back up later tonight.

I didn't know where to find a vase for the flowers. I found a plastic beach bucket and stuck them in it and added some water. The bucket still had a little sand in it, but I didn't think it would hurt the flowers.

I folded up Levi's letter and put it in my pocket and went to find Daddy.

I was ready to see Ellie.

177

Dear Penny,

On the way to the hospital, I told Daddy about the lasagna and the flowers. He said that was very nice of my friends and how nice it will be to have something good to eat tonight.

Daddy said that Ellie was in a special room right now and he didn't know if we could bring the flowers yet. I wasn't sure what he meant, but I didn't ask anymore questions.

When we arrived at the hospital, I went to the waiting room and it was empty. I sat in my corner and waited for Daddy to check and see if it was ok for me to go in and visit Ellie.

I thought about reading Levi's letter, but every time I went to get it out of my pocket, I stopped.

After a few minutes, Daddy came to get me and told me we could visit Ellie. He said that Wanna was taking a nap, so I needed to be extra quiet.

I peeked into Ellie's room and saw that she was sitting up and her eyes were open.

178

Dear Penny,

When Ellie saw me today, she smiled. The tube in her mouth was gone. She picked up her little hand and tried to wave, but I think she was still too tired.

Wanna was sleeping on a little bed on the other side of the room. Daddy pushed a small chair up to Ellie's bed and told me to sit down. He said that he was going to talk to the nurses and try to find Ellie's doctor.

I sat on the small chair next to Ellie, and she moved her hand toward me like she wanted me to hold it. I was worried about taking her hand because there was a needle taped to the top of it. Plus, the skin around the needle was purple and black.

So instead I put my hand down on the bed and she placed her hand on top of mine.

Ellie's eyelids were tired. She stared at me, and then her eyelids would close for a minute, and then she would open her eyes and stare at me again.

When she spoke, I could barely hear her, but it was clear what she said. She said—

An-Ya sing?

I looked at her and said—

Do you want me to sing to you, Ellie?

She squeezed my hand as a way to answer yes.

I thought about what I needed to do. I didn't catch her when she fell down the stairs. I knew I needed to do what she asked me to do now. But I felt worried that I would try and nothing would come out. Plus, the machines in the room beeped a lot, and I didn't know if I could concentrate.

So I said—

I will try Ellie, but it might not be very good.

She squeezed my hand again to tell me that it was ok.

The only song I could think of to sing was the 'Fly Away' song. I listened to it many times on Wanna's music player, and I knew the words in my head.

When I started singing, the first words came out like I was talking. Then I closed my eyes and kept going. By the time I reached the middle of the song, it began to come out of me the way that I wanted it to. I didn't hear any of the machines. It was like they stopped making noises to let me sing.

Finally, I sang the last words—

For you are a sweet child with bright sunny eyes,

A gem of the earth as you soar through the sky.

Fly away, fly away, fly away.

And slowly I opened my eyes. Ellie was smiling at me and squeezed my hand. She whispered—

An-Ya, pretty song.

Then it felt like there were other eyes looking at me. I turned to see Daddy standing in the doorway and smiling. He was looking toward the other side of the room. I turned the other way where Daddy was looking. Wanna was lying in her small bed, but her eyes were open and she was smiling too.

Then a nurse, who was short but her belly was big, came into the room and asked me if I could move my chair. She said she needed to take a closer look at Ellie.

The nurse said to me—

If you could scoot a bit out of the way dear? I want to make sure your sweet little sister is doing as perfect as we think she is doing!

I stood up and walked past Daddy, out of Ellie's room, and went back to the waiting room.

179

Dear Penny,

On the car ride home from the hospital, I asked Daddy why Ellie's hand was purple and black. He said that her hand was bruised from the poking needles, but that once the needles weren't in her hand anymore that her skin would heal.

It was dark in the car except for the other car lights that shined inside our car as they passed by.

Usually Daddy listened to the car radio, but it wasn't turned on tonight.

Daddy said—

Ellie should be moved to a regular room in the hospital tomorrow.

I said—

Ok.

He said—

That means that she can have flowers in her room.

I said—

Ok. I will bring her the flowers tomorrow.

Daddy was quiet after that.

I asked—

How long will it take for the hole in Ellie's head to grow back?

He said—

I don't know. I haven't asked the doctors that exact question. Maybe your mother knows.

There was silence after that until Daddy said—

An-Ya, your singing voice is beautiful.

I said—

Do you think the bones in her head will grow all the way back to the same as before?

Daddy said—

I don't know, An-Ya. I hope so.

180

Dear Penny,

Sitka came over for dinner and she was carrying a bag. Daddy called her parents earlier and asked them if Sitka could sleep over again. He didn't ask me first. He told me that he thought it would be good for me to have company while Wanna and Ellie were at the hospital. I wanted to tell him that I would rather be alone and curl up with Angel Bones. But I didn't say anything.

We ate Jazz's lasagna. It smelled very good, but I wasn't hungry and ate a small piece. Sitka ate two big pieces and said it was the best lasagna she ever tasted.

Daddy helped me find a big vase to put Lex and Levi's flowers in until I could take them to the hospital tomorrow. I want to give Ellie all the flowers because she needs them more than I do right now. Sitka talked a lot about how beautiful the flowers were and how nice it was that Lex and Levi gave them to us.

181

Dear Penny,

Sitka is asleep in my bed. We talked some before she fell asleep.

First, as we were changing into our pajamas, I remembered Levi's letter in my pocket. I don't know how I could have forgotten about it. I pulled it out and stared at the envelope. Sitka saw me and asked me what it was. When I told her it was a letter from Levi, she started clapping in the same way that Ellie claps when she is excited.

I told Sitka that Levi gave it to me this morning but I forgot I had it. Sitka seemed surprised that I would forget something so big. She asked me if I was going to open it. I said I didn't know and finished putting my pajamas on.

Sitka and I got into my bed and pulled my blue covers against our chins. I still held Levi's letter in my hand. Sitka said—

I think you need to read it.

I said—

What if it says something bad?

Sitka told me that I was being crazy. She said that Levi wouldn't come over and give me flowers and also give me a letter that said something awful.

I wanted to wait until I was alone to read it, but I couldn't wait.

I sat up and tore open the envelope. Sitka sat up with me. We read the letter out loud together. My lamp on the table next to Sitka shined on the letter. It said—

Hi,

I am sorry that your sister had an accident and is in the hospital. I hope you are ok and that your sister will be ok.

If you want to talk about things later, I totally will be there.

Bye,

Levi

P.S. I wrote you another letter but I put it in the trash because it seemed kind of stupid after what happened to Ellie.

Sitka and I read the letter out loud two times before we talked about what it might mean.

Sitka put her arm around my shoulder and said—

I think it is good. He is saying that he wants to be there for you during this tough time.

I said—

What does the P.S. mean?

Sitka said—

It is like when someone finishes their letter and then they realize they have something else that they want to add.

I didn't know what to say. It was a nice letter. But it was short and I wished that I could read the letter that Levi threw in the trash instead. Maybe the trashed one was a little longer.

Sitka said—

Are you ok?

I said—

I am ok. I was thinking about other things.

Sitka asked—

What things are you thinking about?

I asked Sitka to please turn the lamp off.

In the dark I thought about how to answer Sitka's question.

Sitka asked again—

What things are you thinking about, An-Ya?

I said—

I am thinking about Ellie's family in China.

Sitka said—

What do you mean?

I said—

I am thinking about how they would feel if they knew about Ellie's accident.

Sitka said—

Does it matter how they would feel? I mean, they gave her away. She is lucky to have your family now.

I felt my body tighten and I wanted to jump out of my bed.

I said—

So you think we are lucky? You think we are lucky to not know anything about who our family was before now? How does that make us lucky?

I listened to Sitka breathing. One of her legs was resting over mine. I wanted to kick it off of me. My bed was big enough that she didn't need any part of herself thrown on top of me.

Sitka didn't say anything for a long time. I listened in the dark for her answer and wished that I hadn't said anything in the first place.

Finally she said—

You are right. Lucky is the wrong word.

And then Sitka said—

I'm sorry. Forget what I said.

Sitka leaned her head next to mine, and I felt her hair fall across my ear.

Then she whispered into the dark—

Remember how I needed to see that star? I think it was because me seeing and wishing on that star was going to be a part of Ellie getting better. It all makes more sense now. I sure did get in big trouble, but it was worth it.

And then she fell asleep.

182

Dear Penny,

Ellie looked better today. Her face was looking less puffy. She was in her new room and there weren't as many beeping machines.

She clapped a little when she saw the flowers. At first she thought the flowers were from me, but then I explained that they were from Levi and his big brother.

Ellie nodded and said—

Ohhh. Levi with rabbit eyes?

I told Ellie yes. Wanna looked surprised that Levi would do something nice. She doesn't understand him at all.

Wanna looked better today too. She must have used her makeup bag that we brought from home. She wasn't so pale, her cheeks looked pink, and her lips were shiny.

Sitka came to the hospital with us. Her parents were both working today. She talked to Ellie and told her funny stories. I wanted to go to the waiting room, but I stayed and listened and walked around Ellie's room.

Ellie moved around more and was even able to laugh. I guess I should be thankful to Sitka that she was able to make Ellie giggle and help Ellie forget that she was in a hospital room with a hole in her head.

Levi and Lex's flowers were not the only flowers in the room. There were a few baskets filled with flowers too. Plus, there were cards hung up on a board from Wanna and Daddy's friends and some of their relatives that I never knew existed. Who are Cousin Danny and Great Auntie Gladys?

183

Dear Penny,

We didn't stay at the hospital for very long today. Daddy said that he had to go to work and take care of a few things. He asked me if I wanted to stay at the hospital or go home.

I told him that I wanted to go home. Sitka was going to stay until her parents were finished with their work at the hospital. Sitka said she planned on staying with Ellie until it was time for her to go home with her parents.

I told Daddy that I was tired. It was true. I haven't been sleeping well.

When I said goodbye to Wanna, she buried her face into my hair and breathed in deep. It was like she was trying to smell inside of me.

She whispered into my hair—

I miss you.

184

Dear Penny,

Daddy dropped me off at the house and told me to lock the door behind me. He said that all of the emergency numbers were on the fridge and to call him if I was worried about anything.

It was my first time in the house by myself. I don't remember ever being totally alone before. I guess I was alone when She left us in the box together, but I don't remember that.

I did have Angel Bones. She seemed upset about all of the time she was spending alone. Her head was hanging down, and her tail wasn't wagging as fast as it usually does.

I took her outside for a quick walk around the yard. Then I went inside and locked the door behind me like Daddy told me to.

Angel Bones followed me upstairs to my bedroom. I still didn't feel comfortable walking on the stairs. I kept picturing Ellie falling down each stair that I walked up.

I thought that I wanted to sleep. I took off my shoes and pants and crawled into bed. Angel Bones jumped up and curled up next to me. I pet her soft white fur and talked to her. I told her why we have been gone a lot and told her that I was sorry that we have been leaving her for long times alone.

Angel Bones licked my hand to tell me that she forgave me. It felt like she understood.

I thought that I would fall asleep, but I closed my eyes and opened them a few minutes later.

My first thought was—

I am alone in the house and I could do anything that I want to do. I could go crazy if I wanted to and nobody would know about it. I could take whatever I want from whoever I want to.

185

Dear Penny,

Am I terrible? What was wrong with me and my brain that I was thinking of all of the bad things that I could do?

I couldn't fall asleep.

I kept thinking about how dirty the kitchen was. Nobody had cleaned anything since Ellie's fall. Wanna never left the kitchen dirty.

There were dishes piled in the sink. There was trash all over the counter.

I know Wanna doesn't like me doing cleaning things, but I had to do something or I worried I might do something worse.

I put my pants back on and went back downstairs. Angel Bones jumped out of bed and followed me.

I went to the cabinet where Wanna kept her cleaning supplies. I watched her open the cabinet many times, but I never looked inside myself before.

First I found Wanna's orange cleaning gloves. I tried them on, and they kept slipping off every time I tried to pick something up. How does she get anything done with those gloves on her hands?

I put the gloves back and decided to clean without any gloves. I didn't wear gloves in China, and I am not sure how they are supposed to help.

Inside the cleaning cabinet were so many bottles and each one of the bottles did something different—

1. Window Cleaner (for windows only?)

2. Wood Cleaner (but do not use on wood floors! It was the lemon smelling one that Wanna used a lot)

3. Wood Cleaner (only for wood floors!)

4. Dishwashing Soap (but don't use in dishwasher!)

5. Dishwashing Soap (but only for using in dishwasher!)

6. Antibacterial Cleaner (?)

7. All Purpose Cleaner (?)

8. Tub and Tile Cleaner

9. Toilet Cleaner

10. Bleach (?)

11. Air Deodorizer (?)

I was confused and all I had done so far was try on big orange gloves and read labels.

I let Angel Bones smell all of the bottles. Some of them she liked, but some of them she barked at.

I wanted to give up and I hadn't even started. I decided to try harder to focus and study the labels. Finally I decided that I would use #4 the dishwashing soap (that wasn't supposed to be used in the dish-washer) and #7 the all purpose cleaner. It said that it killed viruses and germs. I didn't want Ellie to get a virus in her hole and get brain sick. The all purpose cleaner said that it was good for cleaning sinks, cabinets, counters, sinks and fiberglass fixtures (?).

Those two bottles were enough to help me clean the kitchen.

First I used #4 and cleaned all of the dishes the way that I used to in China. We didn't have dishwashers in China, and sometimes I would be asked to help clean in the kitchen. Everything we did there we did with our hands. I liked being asked to clean in China. It made me feel like somebody thought I was helpful.

I don't know how we used so many dishes in just a few days. The lasagna was hard to scrub off of the glass tray. It took the longest to get clean. When I finished, I found a towel and dried the dishes and put them away.

Using the #7 all purpose cleaner was not as familiar. I tried using the spray bottle to clean the counters, but nothing came out. I eventually discovered that I had to twist the spray bottle nose before it would work. There were little word directions I hadn't noticed—
spray, stream, off.

Once I figured it out, I started spraying. I used another towel to wipe the counters, the cabinets, and the stove.

When I was finished, the kitchen looked clean and I was tired again.

Angel Bones and I went back to bed. I took my pants back off and pulled the covers up to my chin. I could feel that my hands were wrinkled.

Right now I am thinking about the many times my hands felt this way in China. My head is filled with memories, but I just want to sleep.

186

Dear Penny,

I fell asleep before Daddy got home last night and woke up this morning hungry. When I went downstairs, Daddy made me breakfast and told me that Ellie is coming home tomorrow. He thanked me for cleaning the kitchen and said that I did such a good job that he was hoping that I would be good at doing laundry too. I told him that I only knew how to wash laundry in a bucket and hang it up to dry. He said that he would teach me how to use our washing and drying machines.

I asked Daddy if we could get some balloons to surprise Ellie when she comes home. He thought it was a great idea and asked me if I would pick the balloon colors.

He said—

Men aren't always good with picking colors. I can design a great house, but I am not the right guy to pick out the paint colors.

Today we will wash Ellie's sheets and blankets and clean up her room. I think we should use the all purpose cleaner in her room too. We should kill all the viruses and germs to make sure that she will be safe.

I am not excited about the balloons, even though they were my idea. But, I am sure Ellie will like them. It seems like we should have something special for her since she lived through having a bruised brain, having a hole put in her head, and needles poking into her hands. Plus, she has lived in a room with all of those machines beeping all of the time. I don't know how she has been able to sleep.

I have a lot to do today. First, I need to take a shower. My hair is sticking to my neck.

187

Dear Penny,

Daddy and I spent the day cleaning. We didn't visit the hospital because Ellie was having tests done to make sure that she was really to come home. Daddy was on the phone a lot talking to Wanna.

Learning how to use the washing and drying machine was easier than I thought it would be. You stuff clothes into the washer and push buttons and add the cleaner. The dryer dried everything very fast. I folded and hung the clothes back in the closets.

Before I put the sheets back on the beds, I pulled them out of the dryer and wrapped them around my body. The sheets were warm, and they made me feel like I was taking a bath without getting wet.

188

Dear Penny,

Tonight I heard Daddy talking to Wanna on the phone at the hospital. I don't know what Wanna was saying since I could only hear what Daddy said back. He didn't know I was listening.

He was telling Wanna what a great helper I was and that I cleaned the kitchen.

Wanna said something and then he said—

What do you mean you don't want her to clean anything?

Then Wanna said something else and Daddy said—

She did a great job. An-Ya seemed happy about helping.

Wanna said something back and Daddy said—

Honey, An-Ya is fine and she did a good job. Cleaning is not going to hurt her in any way. She is trying to help. You should feel better about this, not worried about it.

Wanna must have talked for a minute because Daddy was silent. Finally, he said—

We are good. Everything here is ok. An-Ya was just trying to help. Stop worrying about things that you don't need to be worried about. Give Ellie a kiss from me. Get some sleep.

I hope Wanna understood what Daddy was trying to tell her. I like cleaning and it is nothing for her to worry about.

189

Dear Penny,

It is the middle of the night. I was dreaming and it was terrible. I woke up wanting to scream.

In the dream I was by myself and it was dark. I was walking by the lake. I tripped on something and fell into the water, but I couldn't move my arms and legs to swim. I sank down deep into the lake. For some reason I couldn't move at all. Water started getting into my mouth and choking me. Then I woke up.

I am awake now but still feel like I can't breathe.

Daddy is asleep in his room. I can hear him snoring. If Wanna was here, she would have heard me wake up.

I need to try and go back to sleep. Ellie is coming home tomorrow.

190

Dear Penny,

This morning Daddy drove me to a store called Party Hearty. It is a store that has everything for any kind of party that you could think of.

Daddy gave me twenty dollars and told me to go buy the balloons. He said he was going into the grocery store next to the party store. He wanted to buy some food for tonight.

I walked into Party Hearty, and I didn't know where to begin to look. The store made me uncomfortable. It made my eyes hurt. Everything in the store was too bright. My eyes couldn't focus. All I wanted to get were balloons, but all I saw were costumes and masks and plates and signs and wedding candles.

I was about to walk out of the store and wait for Daddy when a big woman with a little voice said—

Can I help you?

I almost pretended I didn't hear her. I almost walked away. Instead I said—

I need brain surgery balloons.

The big woman looked at me and blinked a few times before she said—

Can you explain to me again how I can help you?

I told her that my sister fell down the stairs and had brain surgery and she was feeling better and coming home and I wanted to give her balloons to make her feel better.

I was sure that the big woman didn't understand what I said because I wasn't even sure what I said. But then she blinked at me a few more times and said—

I see. Well, follow me and we will get you exactly what you need.

She took me to a corner of the store that was filled with flat balloons in every color. She asked me what color my sister liked the best, and I told her pink. She asked me what color I liked the best, and I told her blue. Then she said that pink and blue would look lovely with orange mixed in.

She took the flat pink, blue, and orange balloons and filled them all up on a balloon machine. At the bottom of each balloon she tied white ribbons.

When she finished, there were twelve balloons. Four balloons in each color. She handed them to me and told me that she hoped my sister would be happy when she came home.

I said—

Thank you for your help.

She blinked and smiled and said—

Have a wonderful day.

191

Dear Penny,

I waited for Daddy outside of the Party Hearty store. I didn't wait very long before he came out with his groceries. I was happy and smiling. I never liked balloons before, but this time I liked the balloons that I was holding.

It was windy. The balloons were flying behind me, and I was trying to keep them all together without any of them flying away.

Daddy told me that the colors that I picked were perfect. He asked me if there was any change. I handed him the twenty dollars back that he gave me before I went into the store.

He looked at me like I had done something wrong. The big woman didn't ask me to pay. I forgot to ask.

I didn't try to steal the balloons.

Daddy told me to wait there with the balloons and he went into the Party Hearty store.

I stood in the wind struggling to keep all the balloons safe and wondered if I had ruined everything and if all the balloons would need to be returned. Ellie would never get to see how nice the balloons looked. Daddy would never forgive me. He would tell Wanna that I was stealing.

When Daddy came back out of the store, he put his hand on my head and said—

That sure was a really nice lady. Let's get you and those pretty balloons in the car and head home.

192

Dear Penny,

I am sitting on our sofa and looking out of the window waiting for Wanna and Ellie to come home. Daddy called Wanna before they left the hospital and he said they would be home soon.

I put the balloons close to the front door so that Ellie will see them right after she comes inside.

Angel Bones seems like she knows something is going to happen because she is running in circles and making little growling sounds at the sofa.

It is dark outside.

I was thinking about the night that the 911 woman told me to look for the lights. This time I am looking for Wanna's car lights and not the lights of an ambulance.

I never want to watch for the lights of an ambulance ever again.

193

Ellie is home. I will tell you about it tomorrow.

194

Dear Penny,

Ellie coming home didn't go the way that I thought it would. First, nobody told me that Ellie would be in a wheelchair.

Wanna and Daddy carried Ellie in the chair up the front stairs and into our house. She looked small in her fluffy pink pajamas and matching robe.

The wheelchair was black with yellow stripes on the wheels. I wasn't expecting Ellie to come home and be pushed around in a wheelchair. The wheelchair colors made it look like Ellie was sitting in a big chair bee.

Ellie's head was covered by the hood of her robe. Her eyes were tired, and she wasn't keeping them all the way open. I didn't know if she could see me.

Wanna told Ellie that she was home now and Ellie opened her eyes a little wider. She saw me and said—

An-Ya?

I said—

Yes, Ellie. It is me.

Wanna pointed up at the balloons and told Ellie to look at how wonderful they were. Ellie looked at them and said—

Ohhhh…my balloons?

I told Ellie that all of the balloons were for her. She nodded her head and smiled.

Then she said—

Mama?

Wanna knelt in front of Ellie in her bee chair. Wanna asked her—

Is the pain coming back?

Ellie didn't answer, but her eyes began to fill with tears.

Wanna told Daddy she needed to go get Ellie's pain medicine out of the car. Daddy picked Ellie up out of the wheelchair and told Ellie that he was taking her upstairs to sleep.

I didn't understand why Ellie was home when she wasn't all the way better. I didn't understand why she couldn't walk in the front door.

I was alone with the balloons and Angel Bones, who was quiet and seemed confused too.

I wasn't sure how prayer worked, but I thought I should try praying that Daddy didn't drop Ellie as he carried her up the stairs.

195

Dear Penny,

I am in my room.

I was thinking about what Sitka said about being lucky to have this family. I thought maybe if I surrounded myself with things from my family that I might feel luckier.

I looked through my drawers to find the gifts I was given for my birthday. I put the sister necklace Ellie gave me around my neck. I put the crystal watch that Daddy gave me on my wrist. Then I put on Wanna's robe and pulled the blue quilt she made me up over my chest.

I waited a few minutes to see if anything changed.

It didn't work. I didn't feel luckier.

196

Dear Penny,

Wanna woke me up this morning. I heard her voice first—

An-Ya…it is time to wake up. You must have been tired to sleep so long.

Before I opened my eyes, I smelled something sweet. It was a strong warm smell.

I opened my eyes and sat up in my bed.

Wanna was sitting next to me with a tray in her hands. Inside the tray was a plate of blueberry muffins with strawberry jelly on top. There was a glass of milk and a glass of orange juice next to the muffins.

Wanna told me that in the hospital Ellie received all of her food on a tray. She said the food on the tray wasn't very good, but the hospital workers always brought a tray for every meal.

Wanna said that she thought maybe I would enjoy getting a tray of food in bed for my breakfast too.

I didn't say anything because I wasn't sure that I wanted to receive food trays like people do in the hospital.

Wanna told me that it was almost lunchtime but to sit in bed and enjoy my late breakfast. Then she said—

Maybe when you are finished eating, you could come help me clean up the dishes?

I nodded my head and she nodded her head back at me. Then she left me alone.

I woke up still wearing all of my birthday gifts. I guess I fell asleep with them on. Wanna didn't mention it.

I think I will sit and take my time eating my muffins. I don't like milk, but I will drink the juice.

197

I helped Wanna wash the dishes. She asked me to soap up the dishes in the sink, rinse them, and then hand them to her. She put them all in the dishwasher.

I was careful to wash each dish well. I was nervous about a dish slipping out of my hands. I cleaned them all and didn't drop anything.

When we were finished, she showed me which soap went into the dishwasher and how to push the buttons in order for the machine to start.

I wasn't sure why we needed to wash the dishes twice, but I didn't ask Wanna for an answer.

When we were finished, she handed me a small towel. My shirt was wet from pressing myself against the sink. Wanna held a towel too and dried her hands. She looked at me and said—

How are you?

I stared at my feet for a few minutes and tried to think of an answer. I said—

Do you remember that time when you told me that our inside maps looked the same?

Wanna said she remembered and waited for me to continue.

I wanted to pretend like I never said anything about the maps. Why couldn't I wash dishes with Wanna and shut my mouth? Why couldn't I say something nice? I could have leaned against the sink and answered...*I am fine. How are you, Wanna?* But I didn't say something nice. I started talking about the time when Wanna compared our inside maps.

I finally said—

I know what you were trying to tell me about the maps and our inside maps being similar. But in order to follow a map, you need to have a starting place.

Wanna asked me to explain more because she didn't understand what I was trying to say. She kept drying her hands, even though they were already dry.

I stared at my feet again and tried to think of how to make sense. Finally, I said—

You have a map. I know it doesn't show all pretty places. You had a bad uncle. You lost your parents in the accident. But you knew your parents. Since you knew them, they are a part of your map. They are the beginning of your map.

I looked at Wanna to see if she understood me now. She kept drying her hands but didn't say anything. I said—

What I mean is I can't even have a map inside of me if I have no beginning. I don't know how I can have a map inside when I have no idea how or where I begin. Our maps aren't the same if I don't even have a map.

Wanna didn't answer. Instead she opened her arms and I let her wrap them around me. My wet shirt pressed into her, and I felt Wanna's dish towel against my neck.

Wanna whispered into my hair—

Just because you don't know your beginning doesn't mean that it didn't happen. Just because you don't know your parents names doesn't mean that they don't exist. They are real and so are you. The inside of your map might have blurry parts. But you definitely have a map.

Wanna put her arms down and looked into my eyes and said—

And you are right. I shouldn't compare our maps.

198

I have been thinking about what Wanna said about the map inside of me. If I do have a map, then it would be very confusing for someone else to try and read it. How can you trust a map that has blurry parts?

I hope that Wanna will let me wash the dishes again. Even if she thinks we need to wash everything twice.

199

Ellie has been staying in Wanna and Daddy's bedroom. They put her little bed in their room so that they can watch her closely. Ellie isn't strong enough to walk around on her own. She can walk a little bit, but she gets tired easy.

Wanna made noodle soup for lunch. She asked me if I wanted to take the soup up on a tray to Ellie.

Do you know why Wanna made noodle soup? Wanna told me that Ellie will need to be on a special diet. She needs to eat things that make sure going to the bathroom isn't too difficult.

You wouldn't know this, but sometimes people need to push a little to get stuff out of them and into the toilet.

Wanna said that if Ellie has to push too hard to get stuff out, then it could be hard on her brain.

How are we going to keep Ellie safe in this house when using the bathroom could be dangerous?

200

I brought Ellie her noodle soup.

She was sitting in her bed and Daddy was sitting on the floor next to her. They were playing a card game called Go Fish.

Before I went into the room, before they noticed me, I stood in the doorway and watched them.

Ellie leaned down to pick up a card and that is when I saw her head. It was the first time I saw her head uncovered since the accident.

I thought I was going to drop the tray. I was surprised that I didn't spill anything. I wasn't expecting Ellie's head to look the way that it did. I wanted to put the tray down and start running, but I stayed. And I stared.

In the middle of the back of Ellie's head, there was no hair. Her beautiful black hair was gone. Instead of her hair, there were thick pieces of black thread that were woven in and out of her head. In between the black thread, her head skin looked squeezed up and red around the edges.

Why didn't anybody tell me that Ellie was missing her hair in the middle of her head?

Daddy saw me standing in the doorway and smiled. Ellie turned and saw me and said—

An-Ya play Fish with us?

I said—

Not right now, Ellie. I will come back and play with you later. First you should eat your soup.

I put the tray down and left.

201

I took you and Angel Bones for a walk. Well, I thought we were going for a walk, but instead I put you under my arm and put Angel Bones on a leash, and I began running. I didn't know why I was running or where I was going.

I ran through the woods and ended up under the covered bridge. Once I was inside the bridge, I fell onto my knees and rested my body against the cool wood walls. When I looked down, I could see the river water moving underneath me.

Angel Bones sat down too. She was tired after running and her tongue was hanging out of her mouth.

I pressed my head in between the bridge's wood beams, and tears started dropping from my eyes. My tears were swallowed up into the river below.

It was quiet. My tears didn't make any sounds when they fell.

I wanted to jump into the river and follow my tears. I wanted to leave you, leave Angel Bones, leave Ellie, leave everyone and everything and swim away from all of you.

But I didn't do it. I didn't mean it. I wouldn't do that to you. I am sorry.

202

When I came home from the covered bridge, Daddy was waiting for me. He asked me where I was and I told him. He asked me if I was ok and I said I was fine.

I don't think he believed me, but he didn't make me talk about it.

He said—

Ellie fell asleep waiting for you to come back and play.

I said—

I needed to take Angel Bones for a walk.

He said—

Do you think you could spend time with Ellie when she wakes up?

I said—

Ellie needs a hat. She needs to protect her head.

Daddy said that he knew that Ellie's head looked scary but that she was ok without a hat. He said that I saw Ellie's head right before her head wound was about to be cleaned. Most of the time, it was kept covered with a bandage.

I told Daddy that I wanted Ellie to wear a hat to make sure. I wanted her to have extra protection. Daddy promised me that we could order some hats on the computer tonight. He agreed that it wouldn't hurt anything to have extra protection.

203

Dear Penny,

Daddy carried Ellie downstairs tonight and put her in her bee wheel-chair. Ellie looked happy but tired. Her balloons were still downstairs, and when Ellie saw them, she clapped.

Seeing Ellie clap her hands made me feel like maybe she would get better. Maybe Wanna and Daddy were telling me the truth about Ellie needing some time to heal. Because if Ellie isn't going to get better, then I need someone to tell me the truth. When I saw the middle of Ellie's head woven with black thread, I thought it looked impossible for her to ever get better.

I know adults say things to children to make them feel better even though they aren't true. The nannies told me that those really sick babies in the orphanage were adopted. Maybe the nannies were trying to make me feel better. It didn't make me feel better. It made me feel lied to.

If the nannies would have told me the truth, then we could have held hands and been sad together. Maybe we could have cried together and talked about the babies. We could have remembered them together. We could have named them together. But instead they lied to me and acted like their deaths never happened. Even Ping-Hao, who I loved as much as I knew how to love, would never talk to me about the sick babies that disappeared.

I know death happens. I hope Wanna and Daddy are telling me the truth about Ellie. I won't forgive them if they are telling me lies.

I am starting to see the map that Wanna said was inside of me. Not only is my map blurry, but it is woven together with black thread.

204

Dear Penny,

I don't know why I wrote all that about wishing I held hands with the nannies and we could have cried together. I would have never wanted to do that. I don't know why I wrote any of it.

I thought maybe I should cross out what I wrote, but then it would make your pages look messy and ugly.

I just wish they hadn't treated me like I was stupid. Most of all, I wish that Ping-Hao could have told me the truth.

205

Dear Penny,

I forget to tell you, we ordered some hats for Ellie. Daddy and I searched the computer for the perfect hats. Daddy said we could pick extra fast mailing so that they will get here in a few days. I told Daddy that the faster they got here, the better it would be for Ellie. It cost more money, but if it helps Ellie be safer, then Daddy agreed it was important. Most of the hats that we picked are pink, but one of them is blue with a purple feather on the side. They are all made of soft materials so they don't scratch or make Ellie's head more uncomfortable.

206

Dear Penny,

Sitka came over for a little while. Her hair was pulled up into a smooth ponytail. It made her brown eyes look bigger. I was hoping that she would come to visit because I needed to ask her some questions.

Before Sitka could sit down, I asked her to come with me right away and sit by the willow tree. She said—

I want to visit with Ellie and see how she is doing.

I told her that she could visit with Ellie later, but I needed to talk with her first. I told her it was important.

Sitka followed me outside and we sat down against the trunk of the willow. She said—

What is wrong with you, An-Ya? What do you need to talk about?

I asked Sitka to tell me everything that her parents told her about Ellie's head. Sitka said—

They told me that she needed time to get better, but there was nothing to worry about. Why? Did something happen?

Sitka looked worried. Her big eyes got bigger. I said—

Do your parents ever tell you something because you are a kid and they don't want to make you upset?

Sitka answered right away—

No. Why would they do that? Do your parents do that?

I thought about my answer before I said it. There was no wind and the leaves of the willow were still.

I said to Sitka—

I don't think they do…but I don't know how to know for sure.

Sitka pushed herself up against the willow tree. She stood over me and said—

You need to stop stressing out. Ellie will be fine and nobody is lying about anything. Ok?

I leaned against the tree and didn't say anything.

Sitka left and walked back into our house without me. I wanted to turn and wrap my arms around the trunk of the willow, but I didn't.

207

Dear Penny,

When I went inside the house, I found Sitka, Wanna, and Ellie in Wanna's bathroom. Ellie was in her bee chair. She had a white bandage that covered the top of her head and went down to her ears. It looked like she was wearing a white rainbow on her head.

Everyone was laughing, and they were all looking at each other in the big bathroom mirror.

I turned to leave, but Ellie saw me. She cried out—

An-Ya! We do your makeup too!

I turned back and saw the things in Wanna's makeup bag were spread out on the bathroom counter.

Ellie's lips were a light shade of purple, and her eyelids were a matching darker purple. Sitka's lips were a shiny cherry color, and her eyelids were colored with a darker golden brown than her eyes.

Wanna said to me—

Come and join us. Sit here.

Wanna pointed to a little bench in front of her bathroom mirror. She waved her hand for me to come and told me to sit down.

I wanted to leave, but Ellie asked me to stay. I sat down on the bench and waited to see what would happen next.

Wanna, Ellie, and Sitka told me to close my eyes. They said that they were going to work makeup magic.

I never wore makeup before. I never thought about wearing makeup before. It was hard to keep my eyes closed. My back felt uncomfortable sitting on the bathroom bench. There was nothing to lean against. I felt like my back was floating, and I wished that I could lay my head down on my knees and give my back some rest.

I felt brushes sweep against my face. I listened to them discuss what colors to use. Ellie and Sitka wanted green for my eyes, but Wanna thought blue would be best.

They all came so close that I felt them breathing into my skin.

Ellie's bee chair bumped against my leg, but I kept quiet. Someone painted my lips with a color that smelled like apples.

Finally Wanna said that they were finished and told me to open my eyes.

I opened my eyes, but I needed to blink a few times before I could see clearly.

I recognized everyone around me before I saw that I was there too. I saw a stranger in the mirror.

My eyelids were pale green and my lips were colored pink. My cheeks were the color of peaches.

Sitka said—

If Levi saw you right now, he would ask you to marry him!

My cheeks turned from peach to pink and matched my lips. Wanna smiled and didn't seem to be worried about what Sitka said about Levi.

Ellie clapped and it seemed like a stronger clap.

I smiled at myself in the mirror. I felt like I really did look like makeup magic.

208

Dear Penny,

A nurse came to our house today to do exercises with Ellie. The nurse was small and her nose was even smaller. I wondered how she could breathe through such a tiny nose.

The exercises were supposed to help Ellie get strong and be able to walk without getting tired.

I took Angel Bones outside while Ellie was with the nurse.

As soon as I walked outside, Levi was there on his lightning bolt bike. It was like he was there waiting for me to walk out of the door.

He didn't say hello. He looked at me with his amazing blue eyes and then he reached into his jacket pocket.

He took out an envelope and handed it to me. Angel Bones was barking at Levi and hoping he would pet her, but he didn't look down at Angel Bones. He kept staring at me.

After he handed me the envelope, he said—

If you say no, then I will understand.

Then he turned his bike around and rode away.

I need some time to think about what this all means. I will tell you everything soon.

209

Dear Penny,

First, I will share with you the letter that Levi gave me so that you understand why I have needed to think so much about it.

He wrote—

Dear Anya (did I spell your name right?),

I don't want to bother you because I know your family is going through a lot right now. I hope Ellie is feeling better. Everyone has been talking about her accident. Not in a mean way but because people are worried about her.

I am sure that it is hard for you too. I would be totally upset if my brother broke his head up and was in a wheelchair.

Maybe this is a bad time to ask you something because of what happened to Ellie. But school starts soon and I wanted to ask you before it started. I thought that I would see you at orientation, but I guess you couldn't make it because it was the day after Ellie's accident.

Anyways, people at school know that I got in trouble and was sent away. I have seen some of the kids from school this summer and some of them won't talk to me. Some of them do worse and they call me names like Levi the Little Thief and Levi the Loser.

It's not all bad and there are kids who are still cool with me. But I wanted you to know the bad parts before you answer my question.

I was wondering if I could call you my girlfriend when school starts? Maybe you are hoping to meet another guy at school and that is cool. I can understand. So if you could circle your answer about being my girlfriend, that would be good...

Yes ok (or) No sorry

Thanks,

Levi

P.S. Lex helped me a little to write this, but he said that he won't say anything to anybody about it. I just wanted his help to make sure that I didn't make a lot of mistakes.

210

Dear Penny,

I know you probably think that I was thinking about the question that Levi asked me, but you are wrong. Well, I was thinking about that too, but what I was thinking about the most was...

School starts soon.

After I read Levi's letter, I ran with Angel Bones back into the house.

The nurse and Ellie and Wanna were upstairs doing exercises. Daddy was downstairs doing work on the computer.

I walked up to him and said—

I need to get ready for school. I missed orientation. What is orientation?

211

Dear Penny,

Daddy told me that orientation is like an introduction to the school. He said Wanna must have completely forgotten about it after Ellie was rushed to the hospital.

Daddy is making a call to the school now and figuring out what papers we need to fill out. He is making sure I am ready to start on time.

I am sitting in the kitchen and waiting for Daddy to get off the phone.

I have to go to school. If I don't go to school, then I won't be there if Levi tells everyone that I am his girlfriend. Is that what Levi really wants? Me?

Should I circle *Yes Ok* on Levi's letter? I don't know what to do. How will I be a good girlfriend if I don't know what being a girlfriend even means?

212

Dear Penny,

When Daddy got off the phone with the school, he told me that the principal of the school wanted to meet me right away.

He went upstairs and told Wanna that we were going to the school. Wanna must have given him some papers because he came downstairs with a pile of papers under his arm.

As we were driving to the school, I started to feel hot. I asked Daddy what the principal was.

He said it was the person who was like the leader of the school. The principal was the one who made the most important decisions.

I worried that the principal would say that I wasn't good enough for school. Under my arms felt wet.

The school looked almost as big as the orphanage. But the walls weren't white inside. They were all different colors with drawings and pictures taped up all over.

We walked down the colorful halls and found the principal's office. We sat down in brown chairs and waited. Daddy seemed uncomfortable. He kept petting his eyebrows. I don't think he was expecting to do this school stuff with me.

We waited a few minutes and then a woman came out and introduced herself as the principal. She shook both of our hands. She was wearing a long black skirt and red jacket.

Her black hair matched her skirt and was cut short at her chin.

Her glasses were red and matched her jacket.

She looked Chinese.

213

Dear Penny,

I am getting ready for bed, but I wanted to tell you more about meeting the principal.

She wasn't Chinese exactly, but she said that most people called her Chinese. She was born in Taiwan, which is very close to China. The principal told me that Taiwan's relationship with China is complicated. She came to America with her family when she was still a baby.

I asked her if she was adopted and she said no. She came here with her Taiwan family.

Daddy asked her if she spoke Chinese. The principal looked Daddy in the eye and said—

Sir, with all due respect, Chinese is a people, not a language. There are many languages spoken in China. And to answer your question, I speak Mandarin.

Then the principal looked at me and smiled and said—

So, An-Ya, what language did you speak in China?

I didn't know the answer. I looked at Daddy and asked him with my eyes for help.

Daddy answered for me—

An-Ya spoke a small amount of Mandarin. Our guide in China found it difficult to communicate with her because he was not fluent in her local dialect. An-Ya stopped speaking her native language immediately after she was adopted.

I wanted to shrink into my brown chair and disappear. The conversation made me feel like I failed at being Chinese.

This was America. I was at an English speaking school. It was my bad luck to have a Chinese principal.

Then the principal asked me—

An-Ya, do you remember your first language?

Again, I looked at Daddy to answer for me, but he didn't look back at me.

I had no choice but to tell the principal—

I don't remember. I try to remember but I can't.

The principal nodded her head and looked down at my papers in front of her. She turned the pages over and studied them before she said anything. When she finally spoke, it was a surprise. She pushed her red glasses up on her nose and said—

An-Ya, welcome to our school. I will do my best to make this school a place that you feel happy to come to every day.

The principal gave Daddy some more papers to fill out and then we were finished.

Before we left, the principal said to Daddy—

You have a beautiful daughter. Of course, we will need to do some testing, but we will worry about that at a later time. If An-Ya is comfortable, I would be happy to help her find resources to relearn her Mandarin.

The principal handed Daddy some more papers to take home. He said thank you and we left. I held Daddy's hand as we walked back to the car. His hand was wet but it didn't bother me.

I was going to go to school.

214

Dear Penny,

Today Wanna took me to buy school supplies. The principal gave Daddy a list of all the things that I would need to bring on the first day.

Daddy said he could work from home and watch Ellie and Angel Bones.

Sitka came shopping with us. Her parents were dealing with an emergency at the hospital. Sitka's parents gave her money to shop with.

Sitka and I had the same school list, since we were going to be in the same grade.

We read our lists in the car and I asked questions about what some of the things were that we needed to buy.

Like…

100 number 2 pencils

How many of those were we supposed to buy, one hundred or two? Or one hundred and two?

Wanna said that she thought the number 2 part was about how soft or hard the pencil was. She said we needed to look for pencils with a 2 written on the side and buy one hundred of them. How much writing was I going to need to do to use up one hundred pencils?

1 box of Kleenex

Why did we need that? Sitka said it was if you needed to sneeze at school. Do people at school sneeze that much?

5 packs of college ruled paper

I was going to middle school, not college?

8 glue sticks and 1 white glue

What would we be gluing that we needed that much glue?

Sitka said glue is used for a lot of things at school. I asked her what for and she said—school stuff. *(?)*

5 pink erasers and 1 white eraser

Why the different colored erasers? Why do I need 5 pink ones and only 1 white one?

20 black pens, 10 red pens, 5 blue pens, and 3 highlighter pens

That seems like a lot of pens?

2 composition books 100 sheet college ruled 10 x 7 7/8

Again, why the college stuff?

10 Pee-Chee folders

What in the world are those?

My head already hurt before we arrived at the store.

215

Dear Penny,

Once we went into the store and started shopping, it was like we were in a race. We went into a huge store, but it seemed like everyone was circling around the school supplies.

Parents and children were walking up and down the store aisles and grabbing school supplies like they were in a shopping contest.

Wanna gave Sitka and me each a pen to mark off our supply list. I followed Sitka and picked things that she told me to pick and threw them into Wanna's shopping cart.

Sometimes I would lose focus and Sitka would yell at me—

Over here, An-Ya! Pick out 10 Pee-Chee folders quick!

Or Sitka would find something that was almost gone and say—

An-Ya, hurry and grab the glue sticks and throw them in the cart!

Somehow Sitka found everything that we needed on our list. Wanna pushed the cart full of school supplies, and we stood in the checkout line.

Wanna said—

Are you girls still up for some school clothes shopping?

Sitka said she was ready, but I wanted to go home. If it was that hard getting ready for school, then how hard was it going to be when I actually went to school?

216

Dear Penny,

Sitka and I took our school supplies that we bought and put them in the trunk of Wanna's car.

Next to the store where we bought our school supplies was a clothing store.

It was crowded and I didn't know where to start. Sitka grabbed my hand and took me to the Young Adult clothing. It felt like my school supplies, and now my clothes, were all telling me that I needed to grow up and get ready to be an adult. What happened to being 12 years old and not having to buy college paper and young adult clothes? What happened to being a kid?

I don't know what was wrong with me but I didn't enjoy shopping at all. Sitka and Wanna picked out clothes for me to try on. I followed along like I did when I bought the school supplies.

Sitka pulled me into a dressing room and Wanna waited outside for us.

Sitka gave me the clothes in my size to try on. I hung them all on a hook. I didn't feel comfortable sharing the same room as Sitka and taking my clothes off. Sitka didn't seem to mind, and she started throwing her clothes off and trying on the store clothes.

Sitka tried on a purple shirt with small white stripes that wrapped around her body like Hula-Hoops.

She looked at herself in the mirror and said—

Do you think this makes my waist look big?

I said—

You are being crazy. Listen, I need to talk to about something important.

She said—

This isn't about being worried that people are telling you the truth about Ellie, is it?

Sitka pulled on a pair of black pants with blue patches on the knees. She looked at the mirror and asked herself if the pants were weird or cute.

I said—

No. It's not about that. Can you stop with the clothes for a minute? I need to tell you something and you need to be quiet about it.

Sitka looked at me and said—

Ok. I am listening.

I told her about Levi giving me the letter and what he wrote. I said that I needed to give him an answer, and I didn't know what to say.

Sitka covered her mouth and then grabbed my shoulders and yelled—

Are you being serious with me right now? Oh my God!

I told her to be quiet or I wasn't going to talk about it with her anymore. I didn't know where Wanna was and if she heard Sitka. It felt like I made a big mess and shouldn't have said anything. But Sitka was so angry with me when I didn't say anything before. I wasn't sure which reaction was worse.

Sitka whispered—

Ok. Ok. We will finish shopping and then we will go back to your house. I will call my parents and tell them that I want to sleep over at your house tonight to talk about our new clothes and school starting. It's perfect. We will figure this out together.

It didn't feel perfect to me.

Standing in that dressing room, I felt like I wanted to go back to the orphanage in China and be with Abby. At least things made sense there.

I feel bad writing that in your pages. I just mean life here is always so complicated.

217

Dear Penny,

I have new clothes to wear to school. Sitka and I tried our new things on in my room, and we picked out what we will wear on our first day.

We both bought a pair of jeans that have silver stars on the back pockets. On the first day, we will wear the same jeans but a different shirt.

I forgot to tell you—Sitka wears a bra now. I first saw it when we were trying on clothes at the store. I don't have anything growing there yet to put in a bra. She didn't mention anything about me not wearing a bra. But she did tell me she knew some girls who bought a bra and put toilet paper inside to make the bra puffy. I would never do that. What if someone hugged me and the toilet paper popped out?

I thought that I would be unhappy about Sitka spending the night, but I was wrong. She made me laugh and told me funny stories about some of the schools that she has been to before.

Sitka was nervous about going to a new school again. She said she was excited that we would be going to our new school together. Sometimes I forget that Sitka moved here right after I did. She seems comfortable here, like she has been in this town forever.

I was also happy that she took Levi's letter seriously. I was worried that she would be too crazy about the whole thing, but she wasn't.

She read the letter a couple of times and then asked me what I wanted to do. I told her that I didn't know. She asked me why I wasn't sure. I told her—

I am not sure why I am not sure.

Sitka said the only choice I had was to let Levi know that I needed some more time to think about my answer.

It seems like good advice. It was better than anything I could think of on my own.

Do you think I am going to be the only girl at school without a bra?

218

Dear Penny,

Today we went to the ice cream parlor. Wanna wanted to take Ellie and me because it closes at the end of the summer and won't open again until the spring.

It was the first time that Ellie has been out of the house since she came home from the hospital. I asked Wanna many times if she was sure that it was safe for Ellie. After the last time I asked, she said—

An-Ya, please. I promise you that I wouldn't do anything with either of my children if I thought it wasn't safe. Ok?

Ellie wore one of the hats that Daddy and I bought her on the computer. She chose the blue hat with the purple feather because it matched her purple dress and shoes. She also wore the charm bracelet that I bought her for her birthday.

We drove to the parlor because it was too far for Ellie to be pushed in her bee chair. It was strange to drive somewhere that we always walked to.

I didn't want to go, but I knew I needed to go for Ellie. I was worried about Levi being there. I was also worried about Lex being there because he helped Levi write the letter.

At first everything seemed ok. We took the bee chair with us and put Ellie in it when we got there. Wanna rolled her inside and Jazz was there.

Jazz came over to Ellie and kissed her on the cheek and told her how beautiful she was and how gorgeous Ellie looked in her fancy hat.

Then Jazz kissed me on my cheek too and told me what a great sister I was to Ellie. She smelled like vanilla ice cream.

Jazz asked Ellie how she was feeling, and Ellie said—

Hungry!

Wanna and Jazz laughed and then Jazz took our order.

Ellie wanted something big. Wanna ordered two scoops of strawberry and I chose chocolate with chocolate sprinkles.

I watched Jazz as she smiled and put together our ice cream treats. Her hair was beautiful. On each side of her head was a small braid that dipped and rose to join a larger braid that ran down her neck. The larger braid was tied together with a skinny silver ribbon.

When Jazz brought our ice cream on a tray, Ellie started to clap. Jazz made her an ice cream treat like I never saw before. It had vanilla, chocolate, and strawberry scoops with chocolate sauce and rainbow sprinkles. There was even a giant cherry on the top.

When Ellie started to clap, then Wanna started to clap, then Jazz started to clap, and then I started clapping too. It was a great feeling to see Ellie excited. I knew in that moment, all of her insides were happy and she wasn't feeling any pain.

We started eating our ice cream and then things changed. Lex and Levi walked in.

219

Dear Penny,

When I saw Levi, I felt like spitting my ice cream back into my bowl.

Jazz hugged Lex. I think she whispered something about Ellie. Jazz and Lex stared at Ellie and smiled. At least they didn't stare at me.

Levi smiled at Ellie too and said hello to Wanna. He didn't look up at me. His blue eyes were hidden under his hair.

I pretended to keep eating, but I stopped putting ice cream on my spoon.

Levi asked Wanna if he could speak with me for a minute. I didn't know which one I was more scared of…Wanna saying yes to Levi or Wanna saying no.

Wanna said to me—

Just for a minute, ok?

I stood up and followed Levi out of the ice cream parlor. We walked around the corner, then we stopped and stood next to each other. I began to doubt if Sitka's advice was going to work.

Levi started kicking a rock on the sidewalk. We watched the rock move around on the ground. He didn't look at me, but he said—

I hope I didn't make you mad with the letter.

I said—

No. It didn't make me mad at all. It was a nice letter.

Finally he looked up at me.

He said—

Are you sure?

I said—

I'm sure. It was really nice. I just need some time to think about it. Is that ok?

He said—

Sure.

Then he smiled at me. He has the best smile.

I smiled back but I kept my lips closed. I was worried my teeth might be brown from the chocolate ice cream.

Can you believe it? Sitka's advice worked.

220

Dear Penny,

Tomorrow we are going to the lake to watch the end-of-summer fireworks. Wanna told me every year this town has fireworks that celebrate the end of summer and the beginning of fall. Wanna said they are very pretty. I am not sure if Ellie is ready to go to a fireworks show.

221

It is late and I am home from the fireworks. Wanna was right...the fireworks were pretty. It was like there were double fireworks because the fireworks in the sky were reflected in the lake water.

We drove part of the way to the lake instead of walking the path through the covered bridge. Daddy parked the car and carried Ellie to the beach. Wanna brought a big blanket for us to sit on.

There were people everywhere sitting on the sand.

The air was cool, and Ellie was wearing one of her new pink hats and a puffy jacket. She looked like she was going to fall asleep on Daddy's lap. The fireworks didn't start until it was dark, and it was past Ellie's bedtime before they began.

Wanna sat next to me and asked me if I was warm enough. I told her that I was fine, but really I was a little cold. I was wearing a sweater, but I should have worn a big jacket like Ellie did. I sat closer to Wanna to stay warm.

When the fireworks started, it brought back a memory that I had forgotten about. A memory from China.

In China we celebrated Chinese New Year. I don't remember everything we did, but I do remember one year when all of the children in the orphanage were taken to see big fireworks.

The nannies gave the children a big rope to hold onto. One nanny held the front of the rope and another nanny held the back. We were told to hold onto the middle of the rope, and we started walking. It felt like we walked far into the night. Even with tiny street lanterns lit along the way, it was still dark. There were many small streets that we walked on, and we kept turning down more streets and walked on some more. Every once in awhile, there would be a banging sound, and sparkling colors in the sky would light the way.

Abby walked in front of me, but I could tell she was tired from the walking. I was about to pick her up and put her on my back when we reached a large road crowded with people.

The nannies told us to sit down together on the big street's sidewalk. It was loud and I could tell that Abby was scared. She wrapped her arms around my waist and dug her head into me. I put my jacket around her and held her close to me.

When the fireworks started, Abby started to shake. I rubbed her back and tried to tell her that if she looked at the fireworks, then she might like them. But she wouldn't look.

She kept saying over and over—

An-Ya, don't leave me. An-Ya, don't leave me here all alone. An-Ya, it is so loud. An-Ya, make it stop. An-Ya, please don't leave me.

I promised Abby over and over that I wouldn't leave her. I told her that I would never leave her. I told her that we would always be together and I would never ever leave. I said whatever I could think of to help her stop shaking.

I lied to Abby. I left her.

When I looked at Ellie tonight, sitting in Daddy's lap, watching the fireworks, I promised myself that I wouldn't break a promise like that again.

Ellie wasn't afraid of the fireworks like Abby. She cheered and raised her hands into the sky like she wanted to catch a firework and hold onto it forever.

That night in China, I carried Abby back to the orphanage. I carried Abby the same way that Daddy carried Ellie to get her back home tonight.

222

Dear Penny,

School starts tomorrow. I think I have checked my backpack more than 20 times to make sure that I have everything that I need.

My clothes are hanging on my door knob and are ready for me to put on in the morning.

After dinner tonight I asked Wanna if she could help me with something. She looked surprised but said that she would help me with anything I needed.

I asked her if she remembered Jazz's hairstyle in the ice cream parlor the other day. Wanna thought for a moment and then said—

Oh. Yes. Jazz looked so cute. Why do you ask?

I told Wanna that I wanted to wear my hair like that on my first day of school. I asked Wanna if she could help me do my hair the same way.

Wanna said that she needed to finish the dishes and put Ellie to bed, but after that she would help me do my hair.

I am waiting for Wanna to come and get me when she is finished.

223

Dear Penny,

Wanna came and took me into her bathroom. Ellie was still sleeping in Wanna and Daddy's bedroom. She was sleeping with her arms wrapped around her stuffed Sweet Pea.

We shut the bathroom door so we didn't wake Ellie up.

Wanna brushed my hair with her brush. She told me that my hair was getting so long and that my hair shined like a black moon.

She told me that she was jealous because her yellow hair never seemed to want to shine.

I thought about saying something about Ellie's hair shining too, but I stopped myself before I said the words. Ellie was missing part of her hair, and I started to feel guilty about my own hair.

Wanna must have been thinking the same thing because she said—

Ellie's hair will grow back just as beautiful as before.

I said—

Does she know? Does Ellie know that part of her hair is missing?

Wanna said—

I don't think she realizes yet. She has a bandage on most of the time and when the bandage is off, she hasn't been in front of a mirror.

I said—

You should tell her. She shouldn't find out on her own.

Wanna said—

I agree. We will tell her soon. But let's just worry about creating for you Jazz's beautiful hairstyle. This is your big night before school. We should focus on you tonight.

It took Wanna many tries before she made my hair look the way that I wanted it to look. I thought maybe it wasn't going to be possible to do with my hair the amazing things that Jazz did with hers.

It was hard to get the side braids the right size. If the braids were too big or too small, then it didn't look right.

While Wanna was braiding and unbraiding my hair, she asked me—

Are you nervous about tomorrow?

I thought about what I was most nervous about and I answered—

I am nervous that my diary is running out of pages for me to write in.

Wanna didn't say anything. She kept lifting my hair off of my neck with her fingers. Then she said—

I think I got it right this time.

I looked at myself in the mirror and my hair was exactly like Jazz's. It looked better than I thought it would.

Then I looked at Wanna in the mirror standing behind me. She looked older somehow. There were lines in her face that I never remember seeing before.

She asked me—

Do you like it? Your hair?

I said that I liked it. I told her it looked great and I was telling the truth.

Wanna smiled, but her eyes looked concerned. Then all of the sudden, her face became brighter.

She said—

What if we bought your diary a friend?

I didn't know what Wanna was talking about and I asked her what she meant.

She said—

We could find your diary a new diary friend. They could hang out together and share secrets. You wouldn't be replacing her, but giving her a friend to spend time with.

I said—

Maybe. I need to think about it.

Wanna said that she understood and that nothing could replace you, the diary that I was found with.

What do you think, Penny? Would you like a new friend to hang out with and share secrets?

Thinking about you running out of pages makes my stomach feel like it is filled with rocks.

224

Dear Penny,

It is early in the morning and I should be sleeping. School starts in 4 hours. It is dark outside.

I woke up from a dream. I was standing with Ping-Hao outside of the orphanage. She was beautiful just like I remember.

She spoke to me in English and told me how pretty I was and touched my hair. I was happy to see her but I was confused about why we were at the orphanage.

Ping-Hao said that everyone was waiting for me inside, and she pointed to the orphanage door.

I asked her who was waiting.

She said—

Your friends, of course.

Then she whispered in my ear and said—

And…some special guests.

I asked her—

What special guests?

She whispered again—

Your parents.

In the dream I knew that she meant Them. She didn't mean Wanna or Daddy. She meant They were here to see me.

Ping-Hao opened the orphanage door and there was a bright light inside. I couldn't see anything.

Then I woke up.

In the dream I was afraid, but I still wanted to go inside.

I have questions that only They can answer. Maybe I live on the other side of the world now, but the questions are still inside of me.

Everything keeps changing but my questions are the same.

I wish summer could last a little longer. I want the morning to stop coming.

I feel like I need more time before I go to school. I thought I was ready, but now I am not sure anymore.

I don't want to leave you and Ellie and Angel Bones. Every day I will come home from school, but every morning I will have to say goodbye.

I am going to get Levi's letter and circle my answer. He deserves an answer to his question too. It doesn't feel fair to make him wait any longer.

225

Dear Penny,

I survived my first day of school. Nobody warned me about school lockers. They are for keeping your school things in. Everyone gets their own locker, but they are almost impossible to open. At least I wasn't the only one who was having locker problems today. Sitka couldn't figure out how to open hers either. The principal had to help us.

I knew it would be hard to say goodbye to everyone this morning, but it was even harder than I thought it was going to be.

Daddy came in to wake me up this morning, but I was already awake. He came over to me in bed and bent and kissed my forehead.

After I got dressed, I went into the kitchen. Ellie was sitting in her bee chair still wearing her pajamas and holding Sweet Pea.

Wanna gave me a muffin and a banana to eat. I took a couple bites of each, but I wasn't hungry.

When it was time for me to walk to the bus stop, Wanna put Angel Bones on a leash and we walked outside. Daddy pushed Ellie in her bee chair and stopped next to Wanna and Angel Bones. I was the last one to leave the house.

Ellie started to cry. She asked me to please stay. I told her that I would be gone for a little while, but then I would come back. I asked Ellie to think of a good trick that we could teach Angel Bones when I came home from school. Ellie didn't stop crying but she promised me that she would take good care of Angel Bones while I was gone.

Wanna and Daddy hugged me goodbye. Then they wished me good luck.

I looked them both in the eye and said—

Thank you.

Daddy and Wanna held on tight to each other when I turned to walk away.

As I walked to the bus stop, I could hear Angel Bones barking at me to come back.

I didn't have to walk far.

I saw Sitka waiting at the bus stop with her new backpack. She looked nervous. As soon as I was next to her, she held my hand and she kept holding it until the bus arrived.

The bus made a loud eeking noise when it stopped in front of us and another swishing noise when the bus door opened up. We climbed the stairs inside.

Levi was already on the bus. Sitka and I sat down next to him. I was in the middle. I took Levi's letter out of my pocket and handed it to him.

He looked worried and pushed the letter into his backpack.

I tried not to look at all of the other children sitting on the bus.

Sitka held my hand again and the bus started moving.

I turned to look at my family behind me. They were all standing next to the willow tree and waving. I waved back, but I don't think they could see me anymore.

On the way to school, we passed the covered bridge and then I saw the lake shining in the early morning sun.

I am tired. It has been a long day, and I have to do it all over again tomorrow. I promise that I will tell you more about school soon.

Oh—I do want to tell you one more thing…about Levi's letter…

I circled—*Yes ok.*

Goodnight, Penny. Sweet dreams.

About the Author

Diane René Christian is an award winning short story writer turned novelist. Her work has appeared in various print and electronic publications. She lives in the Pacific Northwest with her husband and two daughters.

Made in the USA
Charleston, SC
24 April 2012